# PACIFICA

# PACIFICA

Nadine Amadio

photographs by John Tristram

## Myth, Magic and Traditional Wisdom from the South Sea Islands

Angus&Robertson
An imprint of HarperCollinsPublishers

An Angus & Robertson Publication

Angus&Robertson, an imprint of
HarperCollins*Publishers*
25 Ryde Road, Pymble, Sydney 2073, Australia
31 View Road, Glenfield, Auckland 10, New Zealand
77-85 Fulham Palace Road, London W6 8JB, United Kingdom
10 East 53rd Street, New York, NY 10022, USA

First published in Australia in 1993

National Library of Australia
Cataloguing-in-Publication data:
    Amadio, Nadine
    Pacifica: myth, magic and traditional wisdom from the South Sea Islands
    ISBN 0 207 18316 3
    1. Mythology, Oceanic. 2. Oceania - Social life and customs.
    I. Tristram, John Davy. II. Title.
    306.0995

9 8 7 6 5 4 3 2 1
96  95  94  93

Printed in Australia by Inprint Ltd  Brisbane Australia.

**OPPOSITE TITLE PAGE:** *A traditional Kiribati canoe.*

**TITLE PAGE:** *'Kastom' villagers from the island of Tanna.*

*To Ian James Wilson from Nadine*

*To Lillian Alexis from John*

# CONTENTS

# ACKNOWLEDGMENTS

We wish to thank the following people and organizations for their invaluable assistance: Andy Lloyd-James, SBS television; Noel Cronin, Dandelion Distribution, London; Polynesian Airlines for travel in the Pacific; Solomon Airlines for travel in Melanesia; Jadon Color Lab Pty Ltd; Fiji Visitors Bureau.

For additional photography in this book: Michael Dillon, Philippe Metois and James Wilson. Photograph of giant turtle: Australian Photo Library. Photograph of Gauguin's 'When Will You Marry?' reproduced by kind permission of the Rudolf Staechelin Family Foundation, Basel, Switzerland. Photograph of Gauguin's 'Spirit of the Dead Keeps Watch': the Albright-Knox Gallery, Buffalo, New York.

And in memory of Keith Chatto, Juniper Films' partner in the South Pacific from 1970.

We also wish to thank the following people and express our gratitude to them for assistance and for sharing their knowledge and information. Without them the book and the films would not have been possible.

Kirk Huffman, Vanuatu Cultural Centre, Port Vila; Longdale Nobel; Gabriel Bani; Vianney Apatoun; A. Reuben; S. Narua; H. Makrit; J. Keitardi; G.A. Bani; Willie Roy; Chief Isaac Wan; Makrith Naumu, Ministry of Information, Suva, Fiji; Paul Geraghty; Vueti Logauau; Qeta Ione; Kustino Samte; I. Naivalu; S. Tokaiqali; Enare Bicilo; Birendra Singh; M. Tabua; S. Rokobote; M. Liku; Akosita Mationi; T. Dautei; V. Nadaku; S. Senileba; M. Saint; F. Rauviko; W. Rokotinwi; Sala Voce; K. Amelia; M. Biuvakaloloma; F. Mateitoga; S. Nauunisaraui; Poase Voce, Tahiti Tourist Promotion Board; Raymond Graffe; Alain Deviegre; Herai Lehartel; Claude Coirault; Tiki Village; Gerard Taaroa; Victoria Tuiateikiviapu; Georgette and Maurice Maimatui; Honia Dany; Flores Ben; Chief Nathan Wate; Michael McCoy; Dr. Michael; David Kausimae; Anisetto Manengela; H. Fiolo; T. Fiolo; Lawrence Foanaoto; Victor Totu; J. Selo; E. Samo; T. Justley; A. Peli; H. Maxwell; C. Mae; A. Ramo; D. Toly; The Tonga Visitors Bureau; Fafa Island Resort; The Princess Salote Mafile'o Pilolevu Tuita; Leo Hapanoa; T. Savieti; S. Lolohea; K. Kapasi; T. Vehikite; K. Sungalu; M. Legar; S. Lanisi; T. Mila; P. Tengange; A. Ngaluola; Pamela Gilpin; Robert Barlow; Maopa Choir; Malekamu Manu; Western Samoa Visitors Bureau; Fulmaona Fereti. Uelese Petaia; Suleape Petalo; F. Toomalatai; Tile Laumea; L. Laupepe; T. Aiafi; E. Tifaga; Ituala Liva; Falaseu; A. Lio; L. Toia; I. Lesoa; R. Tipa; T. Laupepa; A. Lia; B. Laupepa; T. Toni; F. Puleoni; M. Asu; M. Simo; B. Miscoi; Lafaele; Penoa; Patisone; L. Puaafu; M. Tuufili; Cook Island Tourist Authority; Dorice Reid; Georgina Keenan; Tumupu Tumupu; P. Teariki; Kau Henry; U. Teiatu; Marama Ikike; Penny Terepo; Make Toka; Tua Papatua; Ngatokurua Kino; Tai Aporo Teina; Piritau Nga; Teremoana Paratainga; Tangi Tuaputo; J. Aurupa; J. Akerepani; W. Ngamata; Jack Kil; Asi Lohia; T. Vaburi; Chris Owen; Steve McMillan; Lahui Geita; James Tobin; Anda; U. Tolo; B. Tolo; S. Heigi; T. Doura; K. Riu; Waitea Ataria; Maros Mwaroti; Bwere Eritaria; T. Eritaria; R. Namai.

Special thanks to Alison Pressley and Liz Seymour of HarperCollins.

# FILM CREDITS

## PACIFICA: TALES FROM THE SOUTH SEAS

A JUNIPER FILMS PRODUCTION
Screened by SBS TV Australia
The Discovery Channel, USA & Europe

### PRODUCED AND DIRECTED BY
### JOHN TRISTRAM AND JAMES WILSON

*Scriptwriter*: Nadine Amadio
*Composer*: Ian Laurence
*Cinematographers*: Michael Dillon, Garry Maunder, Joel Peterson, Phil Pike
*Sound recordist and production manager*: Ralph Steele
*Series co-ordinator*: Sonia Poorun
*Editors*: James Wilson, Bill Aiers, Imelda Cooney, Mathew Tucker
*Sound editor*: Helen Martin
*Production accountant*: Anne van Worcum
*Stills photography*: John Tristram
*Executive producer for* SBS: Anne Basser

### MADE WITH THE ASSISTANCE OF THE
### AUSTRALIAN FILM FINANCE CORPORATION

AUSTRALIAN
FILM FINANCE

CORPORATION
PTY LIMITED

# INTRODUCTION
## THE POWER OF MYTH IN THE PACIFIC

*The human mind is the ultimate mythogenic zone—the creator and the destroyer,*
*the slave and the master of all the gods.*

### Joseph Campbell
#### THE MASKS OF GOD

*Pacifica: Myth, Magic and Traditional Wisdom from the South Sea Islands* is not a book for anthropologists. These are tales for everyone. The stories were told to us by the people of the South Pacific themselves, and from them came an energy derived from centuries of oral tradition.

What emerged from the time we spent with these island people, filming them and talking to them, was that the creative force of tradition has not been destroyed by the overwhelming and sometimes brutal invasion of Western civilization and religions. They may have hidden their ancient beliefs, stepped back from them, modified them, but the beliefs are still alive today in the Pacific.

Myth was the creative act of the Pacific people. It was so powerful and meaningful, and so in tune with every part of their natural environment, that it profoundly affected every stage of their life. Myth is the great powering force behind the social, moral, creative and spiritual life of the people of this planet who in any sense have lived a traditional life.

When we reject traditional myths, we desperately create new ones to fit our age, or we create modern disguises for the mythic wisdom of the past. This mythologizing can exist on a fairly banal level, but today, generally, the true and lasting mythmakers tend to be our creative artists.

Myth is the art of life. Joseph Campbell, in his book *The Masks of God*, said: "Myth is the secret opening through which the inexhaustible energies of the cosmos pour into human cultural manifestation."

Myth brings a sense of wonder and awe to life. It is a life-force that combats the futility and potentially suicidal emptiness of a purely materialistic society. Myth and tradition impose an order and a morality on life, transforming the smallest daily act. It is perhaps to the larger scale 'rites of passage' that myth brings most meaning. A human being must be guided

**OPPOSITE -** *The conch shell is sounded on ceremonial occasions.*

through the major events of life: from birth and growing to responsibility, change, maturity, and impending death. Myth is the guide to these stages of growth, renewal, and decay.

Most traditional art is empowered by mythology. The travels of ancestors, the passages of life, the lessons of society, and the essence of natural forces are illuminated by it. Myths are the life pulse of the conspicuous energy contained in the world of art. But myths are living, changing things. Told orally, they develop different versions and changing patterns emerge, and a story told one way in one village will be told in a different version in another village.

If you travel for long in these areas, the stories reach out to you and hold you entranced. They have a real sorcery. The tales reaffirm the fact that within the exciting modern Pacific are woven the powerful myth and magic that are the deepest part of the very substance of these islands and their peoples.

The telling of tales is the oldest enchantment known in the history of humankind. Many are real stories of drama and adventure, often with fascinating characters who are both persuasive and dynamic. Many are tales of the magic that is still very much a part of life in the South Pacific.

~

We were a small crew researching and filming *Pacifica* for this book and the television series of the same name, and much of what we saw and filmed was an exciting and revitalizing experience for all of us. We saw for ourselves that nothing in the lives of most Pacific Islanders, from fishing to cooking, is untouched by traditional beliefs. We saw that outside the major cities and towns of the islands, traditional life still endures. To see the remains of still-living mythologies in this modern world was a deeply moving experience. To talk to people who still yearned for the spiritual force of tradition was exciting, and to see people who still use magical beliefs to enrich their lives was inspiring.

There is a new spirit abroad in the Pacific, one that aims to remember and renew tradition. In a story such as The Festival of Dreams, men recapture their warrior past and tap into traditional energy. As Joseph Campbell puts it: "The sword edge of the hero-warrior flashes with the energy of the creative force." In a modern world where values are degraded and insecurity daily shakes people's confidence, traditions bring their own inner strength and meaning.

But what does myth mean today? On many of the islands we visited, myths are believed and still have a powerful effect. Even if they are considered by the young to be old people's tales they still exist, embedded in old memories, and have an unconscious power. They still give a surprising security.

Myths also function on a survival level. If a myth was created to make people part of nature, this is a way to resolve forgiveness for what people need to do to survive. People who live traditionally respect the animals and fish they eat. They are not destroying or taking, they are being provided for by the natural world. A natural balance then exists, which frees them from many of the stresses that we know.

The early missionaries to the Pacific were often just collectors of souls, who felt threatened by the 'heathen' beliefs and customs of the islands, which they tried to suppress. They could not equate their dogma with the vital spirituality of the island

**ABOVE** - *The mountains of Moorea, Tahiti.*

people, nor could they understand belief in ancestor spirits and the strength it brought.

Carl Jung points out how important that belief was: "Because the ancestors established connections with the spirits or served at tutelary deities." An outstanding example of this is described in the story The Warriors, where a boy learns from a warrior spirit. The leading writers on mythology have made this clear. Mircea Eliade, in his book *Man and the Sacred*, writes that "If a man has been successful in fighting . . . he has certainly got the mana of a spirit or of some deceased warrior to empower him . . ."

In Polynesian cosmology, the concept of 'mana' meant the possession of vital strength and spiritual energy. It meant having the favour of the gods. Those who had mana had success, power, charisma and good fortune in life. Their wishes were granted and they were protected from danger.

Because they did not understand and indeed feared the ancient mythology of the Pacific, those early missionaries made determined efforts to put an end to it. In their abrupt dismissal of mythology, they upset the very balance of life for the island people.

In the traditional world, perceptions were different; even space and time had different meanings and values from those of the white men. The islanders lived in mythical space, where instincts were deeper and sharper. They were guided and guarded—they survived—by the old myths deep in their minds. Merleau-Ponty, in his book *Phenomenology of Perception*, says: "In myth we learn where the phenomenon is to be found by feeling that to which our desire goes out, or what our hearts dread, on what our life depends."

Present-day Christian religions have largely extended their wisdom and understanding, and wisely allow the coexistence of many old beliefs. Some of them recognize their value, and actively encourage the traditional life. The stories Rites of Courage, about traditional tattooing, and The Twilight of the Gods, with its celebration of dance, are examples of the Church's change of heart.

**ABOVE -** *A small coral island off the coast of Upolu, Western Samoa.*

The island people understand the invisible other world much more readily than most people in Western societies, as we see in a tale such as Spirits of the Dead. They were therefore receptive to the spiritual aspects of Christianity, but they also, of necessity, live in the world of nature, the world where most of their mythology begins.

Because human beings constantly create new myths, we decided to include some of the

**ABOVE -** *The oldest traditional drummer from Tomman Island.*

great modern myths of the Pacific in this collection. One such is a modern story of survival at sea, told in The Fisherman and the Eel, while the story of The Fiery Messiah is the extraordinary tale of an invented religion.

Two great creative figures to become part of our early knowledge of the Pacific were the poet Robert Louis Stevenson and the painter Paul Gauguin. Their stories became modern myths. Both men wrote illuminating accounts of their passionate involvement with the Pacific, and both left lasting marks on the island worlds.

Gauguin's visit to the South Seas would, in some ways, change perceptions in Western art history. Stevenson's impact on Samoa taught those people that there were white people of intelligence and concern who wanted nothing from them, neither their bodies nor their souls. He won the respect of a whole race of people who understood the meaning of integrity. The two stories The Arrival and Requiem for a Poet are glimpses of two great modern myths.

Myth is like nature in its force and in the profusion of its growth. When the war of the

Western worlds came to the Pacific, the islanders called it 'The Big Death' and were bewildered by the immensity of its scale. Now the wrecks of the war have already been overgrown by the jungle, and nature has turned these grim relics into strangely beautiful living sculptures.

Many Pacific people today can see what important values have been lost with the coming of the white man into their world. They also see how the civilized world has brought materialistic values and taken from them the real richness of their life, and they are fighting for the maintenance of traditional values as the only way to bring back real power and meaning to life. One sees in the story A Member of the Family how a simple canoe, made in the traditional way, becomes changed by its importance in the life of an island people. Myths are kept alive, deep perceptions are awakened, and a vital resonance is brought into being. In their turn, they become enriched by taking the canoe into their lives. As Gaston Bachelard writes in his book *The Poetics of Space*, "Objects that are cherished in this way attain to a higher degree of reality than indifferent objects."

Today, well-known men of the Pacific such as Chief Nathan Wate, featured in the story The Artificial Islands, and Raymond Graffe, in Riding the Waves of Heaven, are among many who fight for traditional values as the only way to bring back real power and meaning to life. The loss of these values, coupled with the spoiling of their environment, leaves very little in the lives of people living at subsistence levels.

Walter Otto points out the still-living power of myth in his book *The Mysteries*: "What then is myth? An old story, lived by the ancestors and handed down to the descendants. But the once-upon-a-time is also a now, what was is also a living event."

Times change with increasing rapidity. A future in which traditional life could vanish just as low-lying Pacific atolls could be engulfed by rising seas is possible. Traditional wisdom, and myth, are our most precious heritage. They bring meaning to life, and rekindle the sense of wonder that is the very lifeblood of the myth itself.

**NADINE AMADIO**

**OPPOSITE -** *The caves of Atiu in the Cook Islands.*

**INTRODUCTION**

*17*

# MYTHS OF THE PACIFIC

*Myth was the creative act of the Pacific people. It was so powerful and meaningful, and so in tune with every part of their natural environment, that it profoundly affected every stage of their life.*

# THE VOICE OF

**W**ay back in the mists of time, long before white people discovered the paradise of Pacifica, there lived a beautiful ancestor spirit called Tinaicaboga. One morning as the sun was rising and filling the ocean with soft shimmering hues, Tinaicaboga walked along the shore singing in a high, sweet voice.

# THE TURTLE

## THE LEGEND OF THE TURTLE-CALLING OF KADAVU

**PAGE 20** - *In one of the versions of the legend of the ancestor spirit Tinaicaboga, she decided to become part of the ocean she loved.*

Tinaicaboga had the magical power to transform herself. She decided she loved this great ocean so much that she would become part of it forever. She thought of becoming a bird—a seagull or a golden falcon—and flying over the waves, or of becoming a great fish and swimming deep under the sea. Finally, she decided she would take on the form of a giant turtle. With flippers like wings and patterned like feathers, she would swim and fly through the sparkling waters forever.

In that magical moment of transformation under the rising sun, the eyes of Tinaicaboga filled with the sea and the clouds rushed through the sky. Everything glittered and flowed in the fractured light. She felt herself spinning and her body changing. Suddenly, with a cry of joy she leapt into the sea, and in her new form came gliding up to the surface, still surrounded with the silver light of her enchantment.

The people of the Fijian islands were very happy to know that the ancestor spirit dwelt in their ocean, and for thousands of years Tinaicaboga swam safely through the waters, certain of their protection. However, the men of Talaulia became determined to capture the giant turtle and make a feast of her. They set out in pursuit and finally, one warm summer evening, they caught her unawares as she slowly and unsuspectingly swam by. They threw her into a bag in the bottom of their canoe and set off for home with their prize.

But the men of Talaulia had forgotten the magical powers of the spirit and she, in her anger, caused a violent storm to arise. The sky filled with shadows and black clouds gathered; the sea turned a cold, dark grey and icy curtains of rain swept the air. Soon, high waves were beating against the side of the canoe and a fierce wind spun the fragile craft around. The small canoe capsized and the men of Talaulia were flung out into the wild sea and drowned. But Tinaicaboga dived into the depths of the ocean and swam safely away.

She came at last to the peaceful island of Kadavu—one of the larger Fijian islands—and made her home in a deep lagoon. She became the ancestor of the people of the beautiful village of Namuana and made them her eternal guardians. She taught the women of the village her songs and promised to come to them if they called.

There is another version of this myth that comes from the village of Namuana itself. In this variation, Tinaicaboga was a princess and the wife of a chief. She and her lovely daughter, Raudalice, often went fishing together out on the reefs. According to the Namuana legend, the men from the nearby village of Nabukelevu saw the two women, seized them, bound them with vine and set off for Nabukelevu. The women begged to be released, but the men would not listen to them.

The gods of the sea set about helping Tinaicaboga and Raudalice by summoning up a great storm. The canoe was tossed about in the high waves and the men were in great danger of being drowned. The next moment, though, they were astounded and frightened to see that the two women had turned into giant turtles. In an effort to save themselves, the men threw the turtles into the sea. The storm died down immediately and the men were able to escape. The princess and her daughter swam back to the waters of Kadavu and have lived there ever since.

The magic of myth has endured into the modern age and still forms a large part of everyday Fijian life. The power of mythology and the mysterious force of its endurance in the sophisticated modern world cannot be underestimated. Although the turtle is considered a great delicacy and is eaten throughout the Pacific, the islanders of Kadavu would never eat turtle.

**ABOVE** - *The men of Talaulia set out to capture the giant turtle.*

**OPPOSITE** - *The ancestor spirit Tinaicaboga transformed herself into a giant turtle, and the people were happy to know that she swam in their waters.*

Today on the island of Kadavu, evidence of this ancient legend may still be found. The women of Namuana still pay homage to their special ancestor, the spirit Tinaicaboga, and she shows her love for them by responding to their call. Likewise, the women of Kadavu village have an age-old ritual where they climb to a special place above the lagoon and sing an ancient song to Tinaicaboga. Down where the water is darkest blue and the surface is a rippling sheet of molten silver, Tinaicaboga hears their song and comes swimming up in answer to their call. The villagers celebrate: they know that all is well if the myth still lives and the turtle appears. To this very day, no-one from Nabukelevu is allowed to be present at the calling of Tinaicaboga. The people believe she will not appear if any of her traditional enemies are in the vicinity.

In the village of Namuana, an old woman who has seen the calling many times tells a young girl, Tulia, the legend of the turtle princess. Sitting there listening to the old woman, hearing her sing, and picturing the old woman's story, Tulia starts to feel a special kinship with the giant turtle.

One day she visits the lagoon and slides into the water, hoping she will see the turtle. She floats face down on the surface, peering into the depths, looking for the ancestor turtle. Far down below, she sees a large shadow moving and is certain it is the turtle princess, swimming and turning in the deep water.

Before long it is the day of the calling. Tulia is up early, waiting impatiently for the women to get ready. They come in their bright clothes, climbing up the hill and walking along the cliff. There is an atmosphere of excitement and anticipation. In some mythologies, singing will cause trees, rivers and fields to appear.

While the women are calling a myth into being, Tulia watches them from behind a tree. With the power of the legend in their minds, they sing the old songs, clapping and calling. Everyone's eyes are on the calm surface of the lagoon. The women feel nervous with expectation. At last something disturbs the water. The turtle is coming: she has heard their song and will answer them. Breaking the surface, the princess appears, her face and body surrounded by the ripples on the water.

Tulia would like to summon the turtle herself. For many days, she gathers her courage. Then one day she stands on the side of the lagoon, singing and calling. She is hesitant at first, looking round and hoping her friends are not there to tease her. Although the girl's voice sounds faintly in the underwater world, the water glitters as down below the turtle raises her head to hear Tulia's song. The giant turtle turns and, flying through the water, the princess comes in answer to the song. The legend comes to life again and in the sunlight Tulia's singing grows stronger.

Tulia waves to the turtle and dives into the clear water of the lagoon. Very daring, she swims down as far as she can go through the cool, clear water, following in the wake of the giant turtle's underwater flight. Finally, she comes close, reaches out, and the princess allows Tulia to touch her. In that vast, silent underworld— moving through the silvery light together—time no longer exists: the two just swim together in the depths of an ancient dream.

**ABOVE -** *The island of Kadavu, a large Fijian island where the calling of the giant turtle is an ancient ritual.*

**OPPOSITE -** *The men of Talaulia captured the turtle Tinaicaboga to make a feast of her, but they forgot that she had magical powers.*

# THE HYMN OF

**H**igh up in the mists and mountains of Guadalcanal, in the village of Turarana, the villagers are assembling. They are gathering for a special reason and they are bringing their pan pipes with them. Their small band of local pipers is to visit a nearby village to perform in a ceremony. The band leader arrives and the pipers line up behind him. The villagers are eagerly watching for the ceremony to begin, as the pipers dance and play their way to their destination.

# NATURE

## PAN PIPES OF THE FOREST

The island of Guadalcanal is part of the chain that makes up the Solomon Islands: six large islands and almost a thousand small islands and islets. Some 90 percent of the Solomon Islanders live in tiny villages that rarely have a population of more than a hundred people.

The pan pipes are a traditional instrument and are still very much part of the islanders' lives. Various villages and regions have different sizes of pipes. The pipes of Turarana are small; in some areas the bass pipes can be almost the size of a man. The sounds are deep and strong. They are played with a coconut husk.

On the outskirts of the crowd, two boys, Geno and Manele, are watching. Peering through windows and lurking around the corners of huts, they watch every move of the pipers. They are very disappointed that they are not considered old enough to join the band. After all, they had been involved in this venture from the beginning, and had gone out with the men to collect bamboo to make the new pipes for the visit.

The making of these pan pipes is not a secret ritual, although only men and boys make them and only men play them. Usually, new pipes are made for each special occasion, such as a funeral, dance, or celebration. The cane nodes are pushed out with a spear, and when cut to an approximate length the bamboo canes are tested for the right notes. The pipes are then bound together in sets with sinnet, the string made from coconut husks.

The boys may not yet be considered old enough, but they decide that they will be part of the itinerant band even if they are not allowed to play. So, as the band of pipers wends its way out of the village and along the mountain paths, the boys trail along behind, trying to follow the rhythm and pattern of the dance. The pipers knows they are there—it would be hard to miss Geno's unusual golden hair or Manele's curious face—but they try to ignore them.

Two steps forward, one step back, two steps forward, one step back. The pipers bend and sway and blow their pipes as they dance through the forest, up and down the slopes, in and out of the light and shade. They dance their way through the shallow sparkling water of mountain streams without losing a beat. The boys follow with delight, splashing through the water.

~

In the history of traditional music, the pipes of the Solomon Islands are well known, although it is not certain how long they have existed. Pan pipes were also known from early civilizations in South America, and they are still played in the Andes. In Europe they go back to the Ancient Greeks, where they were known as the syrinx, the pan pipes played by their nature god, Pan.

The most memorable use of pan pipes in Western classical music was in Mozart's opera 'The Magic Flute', where they are played by the irresistible birdcatcher, Papageno. In Germany they are still called the Papageno pipes. Today, of course, the pan pipes are widely used in music.

The people of the Solomons, with their strong beliefs in the spirit world, have their own myths and tales about the beginnings of the pan pipes. One such story

tells how they were first made by the Gosile, who are the half–spirit children of women who died while pregnant. It is understandable that the breathy, haunting sound of the pan pipes should be attributed to the wild spirit children of the forest, with their long hair and claws. It is said that one of these savage Gosile children was caught in his forest hideout and his pipe was taken and reproduced by human beings. However, not all the stories of the discovery of pan pipes are so chilling.

~

Geno and Manele still follow the band, sometimes falling behind, sometimes running to catch up. They often pester the pipers to tell them things and answer

**ABOVE -** *Two boys from the village of Turarana, Geno and Manele, follow the pipers on their journey. They hope to become pipers themselves one day.*

**PAGE 26 -** *On Guadalcanal in the Solomon Islands the pan pipe bands are a traditional group that perform at festivities.*

**THE HYMN OF NATURE**

**ABOVE** - *There is a legend that pan pipes were discovered when two villagers heard the wind blowing through a bamboo grove. They tried blowing through lengths of bamboo to make music.*

their questions, but no one stops playing long enough to listen. It is a warm, clear day and the birds are singing. Suddenly, the boys are distracted by what seems to be the sounds of another pan pipe, so different that they are puzzled. They know the sounds of most of the wide variety of birds that frequent their island, but still they look up to see if there is a new rare kind of bird singing in the trees. To their surprise, they see a man standing in the tree playing a pan pipe—a different kind of pipe, larger than those from their village.

Geno rushes up and pulls urgently on the arm of the last of the pipers, telling him to look at the man in the tree. The piper looks around: he can see nothing in the tree but the sun glistening on the leaves.

Then the tree piper vanishes, and the boys can hear the sound of another pipe band in the forest. Their own pipers dance on, not hearing the sound. Curious, the boys run into the forest and locate the source of the sound. They look through the trees. They can hardly believe it: there is a group of strange pipers dancing and playing in the clearing, and their pipes are much larger than any the boys have ever seen before. The music is completely different too.

The boys are excited and fascinated, and could easily stay all day watching the new pipers, but suddenly the pipers fade away and disappear from sight, along with their music. The boys search for them but the pipers have completely vanished. Bewildered, the boys wander farther into the forest, and they come across a gnarled old man sitting against a tree.

"Have you seen the band that was playing here just a little while ago?" they ask the old man. "They played large sets of pipes, and music we've never heard before."

The old man looks up. He is busy making a set of pipes. The boys fall silent with alarm: the old man is making a set of the same large pipes they have just seen. "You mean my friends, the spirit pipers from Malaita? They like to travel around. They just came here for a short visit."

After a brief silence, the boys are reassured. Like all their people, they know that the spirit world is always close and part of their ordinary lives. Now Geno and Manele cannot resist asking questions. "Do you know about pan pipes? Which are the right ones? Who played them first?"

The old man grins. "Sit down," he says. "There are no right or wrong pipes. They all make different music, and all their differences are sweet to the ear. Each villager plays the sort of pipes his village has always played. That is the tradition. Now sit quietly and don't interrupt with questions, and I'll tell you the story of how pan pipes were discovered."

The old man clears the air in front of him and a grove of bamboo, thick and strong, just appears. It is a special bamboo grove, with an energy about it, like a singer waiting to sing. The shoots are of varying lengths. The old man surveys his work and nods approvingly. He is well pleased with his bamboo. Next, he calls up a wind. It comes slowly, increasing in strength, and the trees around them start to rustle and sway.

This is a special wind, warm and strong and gusty, with the breath of life surging in it. It is like a giant breathing or a group of men blowing together. Then, faintly and hauntingly, a whistling and hollow-sounding music starts among the bamboo shoots. It is a magical sound, strangely familiar, and it carries with it the perfumes of the seasons.

The old man clears the air again with his hands and leans back against the tree expectantly. Two men enter the bamboo grove; they do not see the old man or the boys, but they hear the music of the bamboo.

"Do you hear those sounds?" asks one man. "Listen, they are all the sounds of

**ABOVE** - *A man of Turana playing the pan pipes.*

**ABOVE** - *Geno and Manele learn that the pan pipes on other islands vary in size and style. The old man of the forest shows them how the pipes are made.*

nature. Can you hear? That is the sound of the wind in the trees in summer." The leaves whirl overhead and the bamboo shoots sing their reedy song and pour the hot perfumes of summer flowers into the grove.

"And that sound," says the other man, as the bamboo changes its sounds, "that is the sound of the wind at sea through the tunnels of the waves when they are breaking, and that is the frogs croaking and the rain falling."

"And that is the sound of birds calling and singing," says the first man. "There are no birds in the trees. There is only the wind in the bamboo. They are magic bamboos. They do not sing of love or war or the great heroes, they only sing of nature and the rich land and seas and the flowers and birds of our islands."

"We can carry these sounds with us and summon them up wherever we go," cries the other man in excitement. The two men cut canes from the bamboo and blow on them and try to make the notes and sounds they have heard. Soon, they have a set of pan pipes and they start dancing with delight. They rush out of the forest to take their song of nature back into the world, and are gone.

The old man leans back with contentment. "That is the true story of how the pan pipes came to our islands," he says. The boys look at each other and smile. They have other questions to ask, but when they turn back the old man has vanished.

But he has left something behind. Under the tree is the set of pan pipes he had been making. The boys pick it up. It is a set of the larger pan pipes, like the ones the spirits played.

The boys rush out of the forest. They can still see their pipers in the distance, just moving out of sight. They run along the track. Then, they hear a pipe playing again. They turn, and there is the spirit piper. As they watch, he vanishes. They run on and the music sounds again. They turn, and the piper seems to be following them, passing in and out of sight like a shadow.

"He seems to want something," says Geno. "I don't think we are meant to take the pipes." He goes into a clearing off the track and carefully lays the pipes under a tree. The boys watch from the bushes. The old man appears out of the forest, picks up the pipes, and walks off, fading as he walks.

"When we're older, we'll go to the other islands and bring back a set of their pipes," says Manele.

"Or we'll make them ourselves," grins Geno.

They mimic their pipers with invisible pipes, bending and swaying—two steps forward, one step back. It is too slow. They run off, pounding and jumping along the track. They can hear their pipers in the distance, and the birds in the trees rise from the trees and wheel over their island.

LEFT - *The boys catch up with the pipers as they cross a stream. They danced and played without stopping as they crossed.*

# THE PREHISTORIC

*Among the earliest of the life forms that emerged from the primordial 'soup' of life millions of years ago were the reptiles. To see the crested iguanas of Fiji today—spike-encrusted, sharp-clawed lords of a tropical domain—is to step inside a vision of prehistory. The existence of this species from such a remote age here in this part of Pacific remains one of nature's most intriguing mysteries.*

# MIGRANT

## THE MYSTERY OF THE
## FIJIAN CRESTED IGUANA

**PAGE 34** - *One of the world's rarest reptiles, the splendid crested iguana now has its own sanctuary on the island of Yanduatamba in Fiji.*

**BELOW** - *There has always been a mystery about the migration of the crested iguana. How did it arrive in Fiji from its original home in South America?*

The small, rocky, uninhabited island of Yanduatamba is the Pacific home for one of the world's rarest reptiles, the crested iguana of the genus *Brachylophus*. Yanduatamba is the only place this species is found in the Pacific. The island is northwest of Fiji and has another small and inhabited island, Yandua, next to it.

The crested iguana is quite a different species from the banded iguana that is found on many of the Fijian islands. The crested iguana is a magnificent creature. Usually an intense emerald green, it has a crest of black spikes along its spine, which become smaller as they reach the long tail. It can grow to about three feet (1 m) long. There are bands of black and white on its body and the nostrils are outlined in yellow. This astounding reptile has rare golden eyes, and huge claws, which is one reason that they are feared by many Fijians. Some island people believe the iguanas

**ABOVE** - *The crested iguana, once in danger of extinction, has thrived on its protected island. There is now a huge population, in excess of 4,000, on Yanduatamba.*

are evil; some dread the iguanas may cling onto them with their large, sharp claws.

The mystery about the crested iguana concerns its home today. What is it doing in the Pacific when its origins were in Central America, or in the Caribbean, 6,000 miles (10,000 km) away? And even more puzzling, how did it get there? An ocean journey of such magnitude would have exposed the reptilian voyager to dangerous seas and stormy weather. Could the iguana have swum this distance? It can swim, and it does have built-in survival mechanisms, such as special glands that disperse excess salt and nostrils that close against waves and water. However, a swim of thousands of miles seems an unlikely answer to the mystery.

It is now more widely believed that the iguana came by raft. Trapped on a log or a fallen tree, it may have been washed out to sea where it would have been carried by currents to the Pacific. These would have been the same currents that brought the raft Kon Tiki from Peru to Polynesia in 1947, which demonstrated that ancient South American peoples could have reached Polynesia. Leaves on the tree could have provided food and water for the journey. It is tempting to think of the splendid iguana like some animal ancestor hero, clad in its green jewelled cloak, setting out on its frail craft to explore the wide Pacific.

It is quite possible that the tree or branch raft is an answer to the mystery. The iguana certainly didn't come by any modern method because the people of Fiji say it has been there for a very long time—thousands of years. In the Fijian folklore of this area, the iguana has always been part of the people's land and environment, and

**ABOVE** - *The small, rocky,
uninhabited island of Yanduatamba
is the home of the crested iguana.*

is called 'noqu manu manu' or 'my animal'. It is a symbol of the land of the clan
and must not be harmed or killed.

The iguanas must be hardy creatures with a formidable instinct for survival to
complete such a long, perilous voyage. It was perhaps the longest journey ever made
by a land creature across the sea. Against all odds, the species *Brachylophus vitiensis* finally
made it to shore on a remote Fijian island. The reluctant adventurer had come home.

Yanduatamba is a sacred site. It is taboo for the Fijian people and has remained
uninhabited. No-one is sure why this is so; the reason is lost in time. Local people say
that maybe there was once a war there, or it is the burial grounds of a chief. Now it is
an ideal home for the iguanas. In 1981 Yanduatamba was officially declared a wildlife
sanctuary dedicated to the conservation of the crested iguana. Such a rare species
might easily face extinction and needs protection. Goats had once devastated the
vegetation on the island. Now they have been culled, and with all predators removed

or controlled, there may be now nearly 4,000 crested iguanas on Yanduatamba.

Enare Bicilo, a local man from the nearby island of Yandua, was chosen by the people of his island to be the honorary ranger for the crested iguanas. The National Trust of Fiji has supplied him with a boat, an outboard motor, and fuel for the 15-minute journey to Yanduatamba. One of his tasks is to keep a close watch on visiting yachts and boats in this area to protect the iguanas from harm from intruders.

Enare maintains a constant guard against fire, and also keeps a careful watch against the introduction of other animals, which are all potentially dangerous. Feral cats or wild pigs will kill small iguanas, and the mongoose is especially threatening as it has destroyed much of the native wildlife. Enare's main management task is to keep a record of the number of iguanas. Sample trees have been tagged and Enare keeps notes on the numbers of iguanas in these trees: they tend to stay on the same tree and not wander far as they are very territorial animals.

The iguanas live in the forests close to the beach where there are a wide variety of trees. They can be found in hibiscus trees but their preference seems to be for the cevua trees. The iguanas are mainly vegetarian and have a special fondness for the leaves of the cevua. They are sometimes hard to see because their natural camouflage is very effective. They sun themselves in the upper branches of trees through the day, and in the evening they descend to lower branches to sleep.

The males are usually much larger and weigh more than the females. Although the iguanas are usually lethargic, the males can become most aggressive when fighting for territory and mates. When they are angry, their green scales can turn black and they can look most fearsome. Their crest becomes erect and the dewlap under the throat puffs out.

The crested iguana has a very long incubation time for its eggs—the longest for any iguana in the world. When the eggs are laid, they can take eight months, and sometimes even longer, to hatch. If the original rafting iguana was pregnant and laid her eggs in the hollow of the tree-raft, this could have been the way the crested iguana brought a new population to Fiji.

Yanduatamba island has a unique meaning in the world of Pacifica. Here is the living, still-thriving evidence that an ancient species, a reptile life form that evolved millions of years ago, was able to forge a link from the past to the modern world. On this remote speck of land in the Pacific it is a symbol of the continuity of life.

**LEFT** - *Crested iguanas are territorial and will usually stay in the same tree. They protect their territory and look fierce when aroused.*

# THE ARTIFICIAL

*In all of mythology, there is nothing more powerful than the stories of how heroes and gods created new lands. New countries for the human race. In some mythologies, magicians, ancestors, or heroes 'sang' new lands into being. A unique and fascinating act of creation began more than 500 years ago in the Pacific, in the Solomon Islands. On the northern coast of the island of Malaita, there is a giant coral reef extending for some 20 miles (30 km). Inside the reef is a large lagoon—Lau Lagoon—and in this lagoon the islanders of Malaita have created their own artificial islands.*

# ISLANDS

## THE TALE OF THE SALT WATER PEOPLE

The creation of the islands led, in turn, to the creation of a new race of people who are totally different from those who now live on the main island. The mainland dwellers are called the 'Hill People' or 'Bush People' and they have a strong distrust of the sea.

Fearless, skillful and swift on the water, adept at handling canoes from earliest childhood, the inhabitants of the artificial islands are known as the 'Salt Water People' or 'Too i asi' (People of the Sea). They are a versatile and adaptable people who, in their hollow-log canoes, use the lagoon like a network of pathways.

Today there are more than 30 artificial islands in Lau Lagoon. The largest and oldest of these is Sulufou, which is about 220 yards (200 m) wide. There are five tribes on Sulufou and five chiefs. The chiefs and their deputies meet every week to

discuss local matters of concern. Narrow streets lead to the village square where the head chief, Nathan Wate, has his house.

Nathan is a descendant of a 40-generation line of chiefs on the island. According to him, the reason the artificial islands were first built by his ancestors was because of the malarial mosquitos by the coast and the almost permanent state of war with the head-hunting Hill People. One of the great advantages of the artificial islands is that they are free of malarial mosquitos and the relentless persecution of the sandfly. There are, however, both water rats and snakes on the islands. But the Salt Water People enjoy the cool, fresh ocean breezes that are a welcome contrast to the steamy humidity of the mainland.

The island of Sulufou is a small and lively world. It is noisy and already overcrowded, with a population of almost 1,000 people, which swells to 4,000 at Christmas when family and visitors arrive. There is, of course, no running water, electricity, or refrigeration. Fish, which is the main source of food, is smoked for preservation. The islanders also buy pigs, carrying them on poles to the island, where they keep them in pens built on the shoreline just above the sea. The pig is a status symbol and a sign of wealth here, as it is throughout the Pacific. Nathan Wate has just purchased three pigs and has had them brought to the island.

The Salt Water People, although they still maintain many of their traditional beliefs, are now essentially Christian. A large new church is being built on Sulufou; the previous church was wrecked in a cyclone. Villagers expect it will take some two or three years to finish. The priest comes once a week but services are held twice a day on the island by the people themselves. The islanders are called to service by their 'church bell': the beating of a hollow-log drum.

~

There is always great curiosity from visitors about the actual construction of the artificial islands. Chief Nathan Wate provides the opportunity to see the birth of a small new island. Nathan's daughter is married and wants to return to Sulufou with her husband, so Nathan is giving her his house. He is currently building a new small island of his own adjoining Sulufou, which will be reached by a log bridge.

Coral from the reef is crumbly, but the plentiful coral rocks that have lain in the shallow waters of the lagoon for centuries are amazingly tough. These rocks are collected and brought to the site of the new island in canoes. Here they are heaped up until they are well above the waterline. It is long and back-breaking work. There is no machinery—no cranes or hoists. The artificial islands have only ever been built by human toil.

Old men who are experienced in the creation of the islands supervise the work and point out the right place and position for every stone and boulder. Out of centuries of trial and error, a knowledge and tradition of skilled island-building has evolved. The height of the island is determined by the height of the highest spring tides. Of course there are freak storms and tides that occasionally wash over the islands and even into the houses, but the Salt Water People are not too distressed on these occasions: natural hazards are part of their chosen way of life.

When the island is the right size and height, the builders spread layers of small pebbles and crushed coral over the top. Finally, the whole island is surfaced with a thick layer of sand. In time, this surface sets hard as it has on Sulufou, providing the streets and pathways of the island.

Traditional houses are built of logs, bamboo, and sago-palm leaves. Trees are planted to provide shade and help bind the rocks together. Each island has coconut-palm trees and alu trees, which seem to thrive in their artificial environment.

According to Nathan, when the islands were first built, they were fortified and then divided into male and female sections. Most importantly, special houses were built to house the spirits of the ancestors who always acted as intermediaries between the living people and nature.

~

**ABOVE** - *Chief Nathan Wate of the largest island, Sulofou, is an eloquent spokesman for living in harmony with nature and returning to old traditions.*

Nathan is deeply saddened that the islanders' traditional way of life was disturbed and changed by the arrival of the white traders, missionaries, and colonists. He is eloquent about the fact that the delicate balance of nature has been upset by the loss of their traditions. Their situation was unique. Their spiritual traditions had evolved to meet their own special needs. Nathan regrets that the missionaries would not allow them to worship their ancestors. He felt their prayers and rituals gave meaning to their subsistence-level existence and brought a special security to their daily lives, which are lived so close to nature.

Nathan pointed out that most of the recent changes have in some way damaged their simple but balanced way of life. In the past, the Salt Water People kept gardens on the mainland near the rivers that supplied their drinking water. Until recently, they were self-sufficient. They caught fish in the lagoon, made boats from trees that grew in the forests on the mainland, harvested yams, taro, and bananas in their gardens, and supplemented their diet with wild pigs and birds that they hunted in the forest.

Today the Salt Water People are still fishermen, spreading their nets made of string from softened tree bark over the sides of their canoes for their catch. Their knowledge is remarkable: they know the areas where various fish will be found at any time of the year. Nathan, always protective of his people, is worried about the vast amount of illegal fishing in Pacific waters, which has depleted local fish stocks. Virtually living in the sea as they do, they are aware of the most subtle shifts of sea life. He says the depletion of the fish supply is already affecting their way of life in the lagoon.

Today, the Salt Water People trade their fish with the Hill People for fruit and vegetables. The Hill People make the long journey to the coastal marketplace twice a week and the women handle all the trading. Now, conventional money is used; the old shell money has only traditional value.

There is a constant traffic to and from from the mainland as the children go to school and the women, with their fish in baskets, attend the markets. Children as young as four have their own canoes and paddle themselves to school with a masterly skill. The sight of tiny children skimming over the water as if their canoes were extensions of themselves is an affirmation of the islanders' closeness to the sea.

In spite of the inroads of modern life, many old traditions do still survive on the

islands. Bridal ornaments of shells and shell money are still worn, together with strings of the once-precious porpoise teeth. When a new bride goes to visit her future home for the first time, her feet are not allowed to touch the ground: mats are spread before her. This queenly treatment originated to prove that she had not been stolen from her home, but came willingly and with dignity, and that the full bride price had been paid.

Nathan keeps the past alive in his tales. He says that the people of Malaita used to be head-hunters, and they kept the skulls of their slain enemies in very special places, which were sacred. They believed that to have enemy skulls made them very strong. These customs ceased a long time ago, but Nathan regrets other knowledge that has been lost. "The men of our tribe who had special knowledge of magic and ceremonies no longer passed that special knowledge on to younger people—so young men never learnt the ways we followed for generations. Our beliefs changed, our customs changed, and from that time nature changed as well." But the islanders still sing their old songs. There is a choir of young island girls, tutored in the old songs, who perform regularly on the mainland in ceremonies and celebrations.

Nathan and his people long for peace, an end to what they see as wrong values, and an end to the slow pollution of their environment. They realize they cannot go back to their old ways, but their deepest wish is to belong to a world where they can live in harmony with natural forces. Nathan asks quite simply: "Why are the forests disappearing? Why are bombs let off in the Pacific? We felt safe once. Now we don't feel safe any more."

**ABOVE** - *The artificial island of Sulufou is overcrowded with a population of almost one thousand people. But it is free of malarial mosquitos, and in a humid climate it enjoys cool ocean breezes.*

**OPPOSITE** - *Children as young as four have their own canoe. They are fearless on water and can paddle themselves to school.*

Nathan's words echo what so many people in the Pacific have felt or expressed. "So many things which came to us because of the white men don't make sense to us. We were no longer allowed to live according to our traditional customs, and instead of a better life we have more problems than we have ever known before. It would be the best thing to do, to follow again the old traditions of nature."

~

From the air the artificial islands have a rare beauty. They lie in their lagoon like small, enchanted worlds floated there by a dreaming child.

Lands are conquered, invaded, or repossessed; rarely are new lands created. The unusual Salt Water People of Malaita are, in a small way, aligning themselves with the old and powerful creation myths in their unique custom of making new lands.

THE ARTIFICIAL ISLANDS

The Cook Islands were named after Captain James Cook who visited there in 1773. They are in two groups, the northern and southern. In the southern group, the largest and most densely populated island is beautiful Rarotonga, the capital. Rarotonga is a visually exciting island. It has a dramatic formation, with central mountains that rise in sharp peaks and fall into lush valleys rich in vegetation.

The black rocks are found in three main places. There is a small close island called Taa Koka, which is actually a black rock island. The rocks can also be found standing high in the mountain peaks. While these sites are fairly inaccessible, there are also black rocks along the beach—a place where fishermen or travellers may

LEFT - *The unusual black rocks of Rarotonga, the largest of the Cook Islands, are regarded with suspicion by some islanders.*

pass. Strange accidents happen in this vicinity—or are they really accidents? At the time of the full moon the danger rises. Some claim to have seen the ghost of a beautiful woman near the black rocks at this time. They say that to sight her is a warning that death will strike some unlucky traveller in this dark place.

Ghosts are often said to be the vengeful spirits of the dead who must complete the cycle of a curse they made in life. The legend of the hauntingly beautiful Taakura, the moon spirit, who wears a red hibiscus in her hair, is a chilling tale of a crime that burns in the victim an everlasting longing for revenge.

It all began with the fishermen who fished these waters long ago. In those days, Taakura was a simple village girl who sunned herself on the rocks and dreamed while she combed the wind through her long hair. She was the most beautiful of all the village girls but she kept quietly to herself. Taakura loved the black rocks and felt at home there. She loved to see the sunlight making patterns on the sea.

The fishermen rowed past her every day and watched her and were awed by her beauty. They stood in their canoes hoping she would look at them. They slapped the water loudly in frustration but she never raised her eyes to them.

**TOP -** *The vengeful spirit of Taakura is so alluring that some men will follow her out to sea.*

**ABOVE -** *Taakura feels a deep revenge towards the fishermen.*

They were somehow afraid to be natural and friendly with her. It was the local custom that the fishermen share their catch with all the villagers, but they never shared their fishing catch with her. Her beauty was like a barrier to them.

Taakura did not tease or tempt the fishermen, but kept to herself and daydreamed in the sun. She hardly noticed them passing by in their canoes, and her indifference roused them to anger.

The fishermen secretly watched Taakura. One fateful day they decided to follow her. They never had the courage to approach her openly. They followed her behind trees and in the shadows until they saw her sit in front of her hut and take up her weaving. They drew lots. One of them was elected to touch her.

He crept up behind her as she sat involved in her work. She had a red hibiscus behind her ear and her long hair floated around her. The fisherman reached out from behind and ran his hands all over her hair.

Taakura was startled at this intrusion. When she turned around and saw the lurking fisherman, she pushed him away with undisguised annoyance and contempt. Her rejection and her contempt once more roused the frustration and fury of the fishermen. This time their anger turned to brutal cruelty.

That night, waiting until she slept, the fishermen crept up armed with flaming torches and set fire to her flimsy grass hut on all sides.

The fire was swift and sudden. There was no escape for Taakura. Within seconds of her frightened awakening, choking with smoke, she was wrapped in a fiery cloak of scarlet flames. As the flames consumed Taakura she summoned up a terrible curse. In anguish she vowed to return and have her revenge.

Not long after her death, the time of the full moon came closer. As the nights grew brighter with moonlight the spirit of Taakura was seen walking on the beach. She came ghostly at night from the island of the black rocks to keep her dreadful vow of revenge for her murder. She walked in naked beauty in the moonlight with a red hibiscus behind her ear and called to any men who rashly happened to be in that neighbourhood.

Few men could resist her call. As they came close to her she mesmerized them and led them out into the sea and watched them drown in the huge waves. Or sometimes she would smother or strangle them with her long black hair. As they died, she sent them a frightening vision from the fiery memories of her own lost life. It seemed to them, in their last moments, even in the sea, that they were being consumed by flames—just as the spirit of Taakura is consumed by a remorseless longing for revenge. Legend does not tell us if the cruel fishermen were among her victims, but Taakura would not have rested until she had lured them to their death.

Today, belief in the spirit of Taakura persists among some of the islanders and they take care not pass the black rocks if the moon is full. A villager tells the tale of how he saw her once when he was a boy and his horse went mad and bolted away. Even now, Taakura is blamed for any mysterious deaths and accidents around the island.

There are several other versions of the Taakura legend. In one, Taakura was a Tupapuka (ghost) who waited at the bridge to lure men of the village to an

**ABOVE** - *Taakura became part of the spirit world. Some claim to have seen her flying over the island.*

**LEFT** - *The spirit of Taakura comes at night, by moonlight, to take revenge on the crime committed against her.*

accident. In another she was deserted by her husband and died of a broken heart. She came back to lure him to his death in revenge for her desertion. There is a common theme in all of them of a beautiful young girl who suffered at the hands of men and became a dangerous, vengeful temptress in ghostly form after her death.

There are still reported sightings of Taakura, and a red hibiscus has been named after her. Now that the moon has waned, Taakura's spirit will return to the island of the dark rocks. But she will be seen again on a moonlit night, driven by the power of an ancient curse.

# FLOWERS OF

The national flower of Fiji is the unique, blood red Tagimoucia. It grows only on the island of Taveuni, and behind its beauty is a legend of forbidden love.

# TEARS

## THE LEGEND OF TAGIMOUCIA

**ABOVE** - *Villagers on Taveuni, the garden island of Fiji, make the traditional kava. The root of the plant* Piper methysticum *is crushed to a pulp and mixed with water.*

**RIGHT** - *The wedding of Adi Perena and Taitusi. The couple wore the traditional wedding costumes of Fiji.*

Taveuni is the third largest of the islands of Fiji. It is known to most people as the 'Garden Island' because of the splendour of its scenery and the richness of its lush vegetation. Everything grows here, trees, flowers and fruit, all in profusion. A high mountain range runs through the middle of the island and from the heights run countless streams to constantly renew the island growth.

In the highest mountains, 4,000 feet (over 1,000 m) above sea level, is a large lake. On the shores of this lake grows one of the world's rarest flowers, the Tagimoucia. It has clusters of red flowers with white centres, and it can survive only at high altitudes. Tagimoucia means 'tears of despair'. The old Fijian legend tells that they are not really flowers at all but the tears of a princess.

Once, long ago in a village on Taveuni, Adi Perena, the beautiful young daughter of a chief, was enjoying the delights of falling in love. Her eyes sparkled and her face glowed with happiness as she went about her life in the village. Her friends soon noticed the glances she gave to the handsome young man of her choice.

If he were sitting near the kava bowl she would go out of her way to walk close to him, leaning close to touch the bowl. As a mark of respect for old customs, villagers would touch the kava bowl as they passed.

The young man, Taitusi, was poor—not a suitable match for the daughter of a chief—but they could not deny the attraction they felt for each other.

There was a traditional game of flirtation played in the village and enjoyed by young people. It was called 'vakagigi moli', the 'lemon game'. On sunlit afternoons they would play, rolling lemons along the ground towards each other. It was recognized as a public declaration of affection if a boy bowled a lemon at his sweetheart. It was no secret how Adi Perena and Taitusi felt about each other.

One day, while the young people played this game, Adi Perena's father called her to his hut. Happy in her games of love with Taitusi, Adi Perena did not suspect the pain awaiting her. She looked around the hut and saw an old man sitting across the room in a position of honour. She knelt obediently in front of her father.

"I have good news," her father told her. "I have chosen your husband." He pointed to the old man. "It is my royal command that you marry Tuki Kuto and strengthen the ties beween us!"

In those times, it was customary to marry the young daughters of chiefs to powerful older men. With her high rank, Adi Perena could not disobey her father's wishes. But she could not believe this dreadful news. In horror she looked around and saw her mother sitting silently watching. Adi Perena pleaded with her eyes. Her mother saw her misery but was not able to interfere.

Adi Perena walked down to the beach and sat alone, watching the waves breaking. She was desperately sad. She realized how deeply she cared for Taitusi. In the shadows of the trees watching her stood the anguished Taitusi. In those days the people of Taveuni were fierce and strong and lived by tradition. They could not challenge the command of a chief. His rule was absolute.

But Adi Perena no longer cared about disobeying her father. She had made a promise of love and nothing would force her to break it. She could not bring herself to marry the old man her father had chosen for her. In torment, she decided to run away.

Very early, before dawn the next morning, Adi Perena set out. Through the forests and parklands, through the slopes and valleys of her abundant homeland she ran. She noticed nothing of the natural gardens of her island. She started climbing and at last she came to a high lake and a waterfall.

Exhausted and desperate, Adi Perena collapsed. She felt her heart was breaking. As she wept, the tears fell on the earth beside her. As they fell, her tears became flowers—the blood red flowers of despair, Tagimoucia.

Her father, alarmed by her disappearance, set out with his men to search for her. They searched every part of the island and found her at last by the waterfall. Adi Perena's father, who loved his daughter, was deeply moved by her suffering. He was a chief, and he knew the truth of things when he saw them. He held up the red flowers she had wept and saw in the colour and shape of her flowers of tears how dearly she loved Taitusi. It was unusual in those days for a chief to change his decision once it had been made public, but he now resolved that his daughter should marry the man she loved.

The couple were radiant in their traditional wedding costumes. Adi Perena wore the high-ranking sash of brown masi and Taitusi walked proudly beside her. The ceremony was celebrated with full honour.

The transformation of Adi Perena's tears to flowers became a story told and retold through the ages. To this day, the Tagimoucia is considered the most precious and beautiful of all Fijian wildflowers. It is a symbol of the power of love and the unique human gift of tears.

# THE SECRET

**N**orth of Rarotonga in the Cook Islands lies the small and beautiful island of Atiu.
There is a legend in Atiu that tells the tale of the lovers Pararo and Inutoto and of a discovery they
made in the heart of the island.

# CAVE

## THE LEGEND OF TE ANA TAKITAKI

**PAGE 58** - *In the legend of Te Ana Takitaki, a bird leads the lover Pararo to the secret cave on the island of Atiu. The cave is formed of coral and limestone.*

**ABOVE** - *Pararo searched the island for his wife Inutoto. He climbed the jagged coral cliffs of Atiu. The coral rocks are called Makatea.*

Atiu—also known as Tauranga, or Enuamana—is a place where no human lived before the ancestors of the Atiu people. The people believe that they sprang from the ancestor Atiu-Mua, whose father was the divinity Tangaroa. Therefore all people on the island are related. Rare and strangely sculptured, as if by the hand of some god of the sea, the island of Atiu is formed of a rocky outcrop of jagged coral known as Makatea.

~

A loving husband and wife, Pararo and Inutoto lived in a hut on the island of Atiu. The tale begins on the night of the full moon when a special dance was being held, the Moonlight Dance. Inutoto, who was beautiful and graceful, loved dancing. She was looking forward to the dance. But Pararo forbade his wife to go.

Pararo believed it would be a perfect night for fishing and that he would make a really big catch, so he decided to go out in his canoe. He wanted to know that his wife would remain safely at home.

Inutoto made a fire in front of the hut and proceeded to do her work. She knew the dance was starting because she could hear the exciting sounds of drums beating in the distance. The dancing drums roused fire in her blood. She found herself swaying to the inviting rythmns.

In the meantime Pararo, out in his canoe on the lonely sea, was having no luck at all with his fishing. He couldn't even get a bite, and he wondered why the sea seemed empty of fish. The moon rose huge and lit the sea. Pararo heard the distant drumming and was uneasy.

Inutoto was having trouble resisting temptation. The dance, like the perfume of flowers, called to the senses of the young wife. Finally she couldn't bear it and, placing a red hibiscus in her long dark hair, she slipped away from her hut and set out for the dance.

Her friends were all dancing, teeth flashing in smiles, bodies beaded with perspiration, moving with pleasure and energy. They were pleased to see her and called her to come and join them. Swaying seductively, she joined the dancers.

Without a single catch, Pararo felt this night that the gods were against him. He paddled across the moonlit sea hoping he'd find the fish, but in the end he realized it was hopeless and he might as well give up. Pararo returned home from his useless fishing and called for Inutoto. He looked all round the hut and realized his wife was missing. In spite of him forbidding her, she must have gone to the dance. His frustration with his lack of fish and his annoyance at his wife's disregard of his orders caused his fury to rise against Inutoto. He lit a torch of wood and stamped through the forest to find her. The drums were sounding through the night. There she was. He could see her dancing to the beating drums. Like an avenging angel armed with fire, he plunged into the middle of the dancers and forcibly dragged her from the dance, cursing her for disobeying him.

That night in their hut, lying beside Pararo on their bed, Inutoto could not sleep. She was pierced with the injustice of Pararo's anger and humiliated at being dragged off in front of her friends. Looking across to make sure he was asleep, she crept out of bed. She decided she would leave him and find a place where he would never see her again.

When Pararo woke in the morning he felt relaxed and happy. All his ill humour of the night before had vanished. He was sorry for his unkindness to Inutoto and looked around for her to make friends again. But she had gone. He did not fear his wife's absence. When they fought she would visit her brother Ngarue and return when it was calm again. So he set off for Ngarue's plantation.

Ngarue greeted him, and Pararo asked where he would find Inutoto. Ngarue shook his head; he had not seen Inutoto that day. Now Pararo became alarmed. She had never gone further than her brother's hut. He had driven his wife away with his anger. He must find her before she came to any harm. He and Ngarue searched for her and called for her all through the island. They went through the forests and climbed over the sharp cliffs by the sea, always calling for her.

The days passed and still they went on searching and calling her name. Now they were very worried. They had searched every corner of the island and there was no sign of her. No one had seen her, no one knew where she had gone. Now they really feared that an accident or some harm had come to Inutoto.

Pararo was searching through the jungles at the centre of the islands, still calling Inutoto. In despair, he prayed to the gods for help to find her. At that moment he saw, very close on a branch, a kingfisher bird. It was like an omen of good fortune.

**ABOVE** - *Searching through the dense mysterious forest.*

The bird looked at Pararo and then hopped away, looking back at him. There was surely no mistake. The bird seemed to be beckoning him to follow. It flew in small flights, always waiting for him to catch up. Pararo stumbled through the bushes along some strange pathway known only to the bird. There was no doubt that the bird was leading him somewhere.

He followed the bird deep into the forest and finally came to a depression shaped like a small amphitheatre. He stumbled down after the bird and found himself at the mouth of a splendid cave where the Makatea and limestone formations grew like ancient carvings.

The bird flew past him into the cave and Pararo knew he must follow over the sharp coral into the secret heart of the cave. It was a huge, awe-inspiring place with great gloomy chambers as large as cathedrals. Birds nested in the dim recesses and the shapes of the rock formations cast strange shadows.

He called to Inutoto one last time, and out of the darkness of the depths of the cave she came, the wife he really loved. Pararo felt a great joy in seeing her again. They embraced in relief and happiness and forgave each other for their fight. Pararo led her out of the cave. They decided to call the cave Te Ana Takitaki—'the cave to which Pararo was led'.

~

In many myths and legends, a bird with its swift wings and high vision becomes the guide of a hero. In the tale of the cave of Te Ana Takitaki on the island of Atiu the bird, a force of nature, revealed the hidden power of love and taught a pair of troubled lovers how to find each other again.

**THE SECRET CAVE**

# TRADITIONAL
# CUSTOMS AND MYTH

*Myth is the great powering force behind the social, moral, creative and spiritual life
of the people of this planet who in any sense have lived a traditional life;
who have lived in harmony with nature.*

# THE DANCE

**O**n the tiny island of Tomman in Vanuatu an islander is running and flapping his arms as if he were a bird. He runs at the bidding of a heroic figure wearing a feathered headdress. These Tomman islanders are re-enacting an ancient ritual, the dance drama of Ambat and the Giant Clam, which tells the myth of the creation of Tomman.

# OF AMBAT

## THE MYTH AND PRACTICE
## OF SKULL BINDING

**PAGE 64** - *The dance drama of Ambat keeps the Ambat myth alive. In this creation myth, Ambat changes his brothers into birds. Their arms become wings as they fly off to act as his messengers.*

**RIGHT** - *The old man Amboya had his skull bound when he was a baby. On the island of Tomman an elongated skull has always been a sign of beauty and intellect.*

**ABOVE** - *A carved mask of the god Ambat. He was admired for his long nose and the beauty of his elongated skull.*

Ideals of beauty have varied through every age and every country, and on the islands of Tomman and Malekula in Vanuatu an elongated skull represents great beauty. This is not a unique concept. A long skull was deeply admired in ancient Egypt two thousand years ago, and was probably the preserve of noble and royal personages. To this day the famous sculptured portrait of the Egyptian queen Nefertiti (1,350 BC) is regarded throughout the world as representing the height of aesthetic perfection.

In Tomman and southern Malekula the long skull is also regarded as a sign of high intellectual capacity. In Pidgin, the term 'Long-fella-head' means that the person is very intelligent. But the admiration for a long head goes much further than this. The hero god Ambat had an elongated skull, and to have one's infant son grow to look like a god is certainly a profound ambition. As the gods and heroes of the Pacific brought significance and a sense of the spiritual into the lives of the people, emulating the gods was a dedication to a traditional life.

So the ancient practice of skull binding, which has a history in many parts of the world, from southern France to Africa and South America, survived in areas of the Pacific and on some of the islands of Vanuatu, although missionaries forbade the practice and it largely died out. Tomman, with its small Nahai speaking community, showed particular evidence of this custom.

~

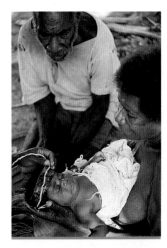

Tomman is a tiny island only a short distance from the southern end of a much larger island, Malekula. This combined area, with its tiny population, has the distinction of speaking many different languages. The multiculturalism of Vanuatu itself is quite a phenomenon. With a total population of about 150,000, the country contains over a hundred different languages. There is probably no other place in the world with such an amazing diversity of languages and cultures in such a small area.

When the Melanesians came to Vanuatu over thousands of years, each group arrived with a different language and different cultural structures of law and kinship. The languages have probably survived because Melanesians are a secretive people. Each clan is the guardian of strong and secret rituals. Each is the holder of certain powers. The key to these riches is the language, so each maintains its own. Pidgin is the only language in common.

Another reason for the survival of this peaceful and truly multicultural society is the respect that Vanuatans have for each other's culture, along with a wish to minimize violence. Vanuatans are deeply aware of the danger of disturbing another clan's spirit world.

Before the coming of the white people the population of Vanuatu was probably in excess of half a million. The diseases brought by the Europeans, together with alcohol and practices such as blackbirding (kidnapping for slavery), decimated Vanuata. In 1926 the total population had dropped to some 40,000. In spite of this, the people made enormous and surprisingly successful efforts to retain their cultural identity. Vanuatu became a republic in 1980.

**ABOVE** - *Amboya and his wife bind the skull of their grandchild. There has been no indication that the traditional practice of skullbinding can cause brain damage or impair the intellect.*

~

Despite the boundaries imposed by language, the strong Ambat legend, with variations, features in most of the mythology of this region. In Tomman and the southern areas of Malekula, Ambat, as well as being an individual hero god, was also the collective name for a group of brother gods called The Ambat. So the name was sometimes used in the singular and sometimes in the plural. In the plural they were five brothers, often identified by a hand. Ambat the eldest was the thumb, and Awirara the youngest was the little finger.

The Ambat epitomized the ideal of beauty in Vanuatu. They had white skins, narrow noses, and elongated skulls. Ambat himself introduced skull binding, because he wanted the people to look like him. He also introduced circumcision.

The Ambat are credited with being responsible for most elements of the culture of this region, plus some unusual land formations. The custom of making effigies of the dead is also attributed to them. These mortuary effigies contained the overmodelled skulls of the deceased.

The creative Ambat introduced musical instruments to the Malekula area, including wooden drums, conch shell trumpets, the bull roarer, and the bone flutes usually used ritually. Ambat also created the sacred Nam-Boi pottery which, large and hollow, have his designs on them. He made sacred stones such as the 'Penis of Ambat' at Iumoran on Tomman, where he is said to have lived and died. His body, which never decayed, is said to be still there, and Iumoran is a sacred place.

~

There are many myths about Ambat, and often several versions of the same myth. When the villagers re-enact their myths in their traditional dances, the stories are like a ceremony. Among the stories are, for example, the Nahave'anti Ambat

(The Dance of Ambat) and the Nitili (The Clam Shell Dance). One of the best-known is the story of Ambat and the Giant Clam, which concerns the creation of the island of Tomman.

In the story of The Ambat and the Giant Clam, the oldest brother Ambat saw a giant clam lying on the sea bed. The clam was sending out great rays of light and creative energy. Ambat sent his youngest brother Awirara to investigate, but the boy was too frightened and returned home. Ambat sent his other three brothers—Awinggotnggot, Awisantwuhlu and Awikintuas—one at a time to investigate the clam. Each time they returned home, too frightened to find out what was happening.

At last Ambat, in annoyance, went himself. He took a great stick and thrust it into the mouth of the clam. The clam died and immediately turned into an island lying just below the surface of the sea. Once again Ambat sent his brothers one at a time to look at the new island. They reported back that first the ground appeared, then the island emerged fully, then it dried out, then the trees began to grow. This became the island of Tomman.

There follows an episode where Ambat grew a coconut tree on the island. It kept growing until it reached a great height. When the brothers tried to collect its coconuts, the tree attempted to devour the brothers. Ambat shot down a coconut with his bow and arrow, subduing the tree. After that, the Ambat took a great liking to Tomman Island. After several more adventures, the five Ambat brothers decided that Tomman was just the right size for them. They moved to the island and made Tomman their home.

**ABOVE -** *A masked dancer on Tomman kills the devil spirit.*

~

One day when they were living on Tomman, Ambat found a fish in a pool. The next day he found a cast-off fish skin in the pool, and a beautiful woman called Lindanda. Ambat married her and kept her a secret from his brothers. She became a part of later Ambat myths, including the legend of Ambat's death.

In one version of the continuing Ambat myth, the brothers discover Lindanda, and Awirara violates her. In fury, Ambat kills his brother and his wife, and he and the remaining three brothers destroy each other. In another version, Awirara desires Ambat's wife and causes Ambat's death by trickery. Ambat intended there should be no death. When he died he gave his brothers tasks that would ensure his rebirth, but Awirara tricked his brothers into neglecting Ambat's instructions. Ambat was unable to return to life, and so death was introduced into the world.

In some versions of the myth, Ambat, his wife Lindanda and his four brothers live in peace on the island and become the ancestors and creators of the people of Tomman. There are also myths of Ambat's sons becoming the forebears of the modern Malekulans and of Ambat introducing the coconut tree to the other islands. Other gods or cultural heroes on other islands bear a remarkable similarity to Ambat. Kabat of Mewun has a very similar series of myths, and Hambat of Lambumbu, much farther north, often seems to be Ambat in another guise.

Lindanda was credited with bringing art to the people. She introduced painting and the creation of other art works, including masks. The masks and headdresses were elaborate and were used in ceremonies and dances such as funerary and initiation rituals. Eventually, the men took them over. Many of these rituals are secret. What is revealed is the public showing of a hidden power.

~

The legend of Ambat's death has been made into a dance called the Nelang. The Neland was danced by men with elongated skulls. The elongated result of skull-binding is termed a 'deformation', but this is used as a term of admiration.

The particular version of the myth of Ambat and the Giant Clam that is used in the villagers' dance re-enactment today tells essentially the same story that most of the creation myths tell. In the dance version, however, the brothers are represented as birds. Ambat sends them, as birds, to investigate the giant clam. Each flies off and returns in fear. The last brother is an owl and Ambat gives him a stake to carry. The owl finally succeeds in killing the clam, and the island is created.

In the dance Ambat wears a feathered headdress for his new bird family. The men who dance the brothers represent birds flying by running, like children at play, with their arms outstretched, wheeling and turning and moving their arms like feathered wings. The giant clam is represented by a curled-up man. These narrative dances are proof that mythology is a living force still at work on the islands.

~

When a woman on Tomman decides to have her son's head bound for elongation, she will do it while he is still a newborn baby and the hard plate bones of the skull are still quite soft and reasonably piable. It does not seem to be a dangerous process. There have been studies made on the after-effects of skull elongation, and there seems to be little evidence that skull binding results in brain damage. In fact, in countries that practise head shaping by mothers and female relatives there is evidence of increased mental health. This kind of head shaping is the gentle moulding by hand of a baby's skull. It is instinctive, and is often done to correct cranial damage at birth.

~

An old man of the village is helping his wife bind the skull of her infant grandson. The old man, Amboya, had his skull bound when he was a baby and now has a 'well deformed' head himself. The long, elegant shape of his head is immediately noticeable. He has been proud of his long skull all his life. He believes it is a gift from the gods that makes him handsome and brings other qualities of wisom and brightness with it. He is pleased to assist at the skull binding.

First, a black liquid is made from the charred wood of the candlenut tree mixed with water. This paint is spread on the hands and gently applied to the infant's skull. It will  soften the skin and help the skull binding to adhere. The skull cap is made from woven bark cloth from the pandanus tree. A strip of the bark cloth about a hand's width and 3 feet (1 m) long is laid across the baby's forehead and wound around the head, coming down low at the back of the neck.

Next a long narrow strip of fibre made from the stem of a creeper is wound

many times around the head, from the crown to the lower edge of the bandage. This narrow binding is pulled tight to hold the wide bandage in place.

The wide bandage is removed at intervals and the black paint is reapplied before a new bandage. This is kept up for varying lengths of time—weeks, months, or even years, depending on the amount of 'deformation' required. The plasticity of the skull of a newborn baby soon hardens, and most of the change of shape occurs in the first few weeks or months of bandaging.

The mother believes that her new baby, with his elongated skull, will be found handsome and clever, and that he will live proudly through his life, knowing he walks in the image of a god.

**ABOVE -** *Male dancers of Tomman perform a dance that was stolen from women. The men dress themselves as women and dance in skirts.*

THE DANCE OF AMBAT

# THE

**A** *pounding can be heard along the tropical sands of the beach on the island of South Tarawa. It is the sound of boys running fast along the sand. They are the young students training in the Terotauea Tungaru Martial Arts and Culture Academy on Tarawa Island. They are the modern warriors of the Gilbert Islands, now known as Kiribati, yet they are still part of an age-old tradition.*

# WARRIORS

## A TIMELESS TRADITION ENDURES

**PAGE 72** - *The Gilbertese warriors of tradition were the proudest and fiercest in the Pacific. It is believed that their martial arts were the blueprint for the other great schools of martial arts that followed, the Japanese Samurai and the Chinese Kung Fu.*

**RIGHT** - *A warrior in full traditional battle costume beating off an intruder.*

It is a time of great change in the Pacific. The modern age of Western values is reaching even the remote islands. Fortunately, alongside this threat to traditional life there is a renewed interest in preserving the cultures and traditions of the islands. The Terotauea Tungaru Academy was established for that very reason. To bring, within a modern context, a sense of the traditional, and a knowledge of their culture to the young men of Kiribati.

The history of the Gilbert Islands goes back into the time of the gods. In 1917 this equatorial dominion became a British protectorate known as the Gilbert and Ellice Islands Protectorate. In 1979, independence was established and the Republic of Kiribati was formed.

The short years of British control barely interrupted the rituals and beliefs of the culture. Today, the Republic of Kiribati contains thirty-three islands, including the sixteen Gilbert Islands, the eight Phoenix Islands, Banaba and eight Line Islands. The total population is less than one hundred thousand, and some of the islands are uninhabited. The Ellice Islands have formed their own republic, called Tuvalu.

The boys from the Academy continue their training, making their insistent body patterns as they exercise. Their bodies are strong and flexible. By the time their training is complete, the boys will be skilled in the martial arts. They will also be inheritors of a complex and demanding tradition, the Tungaru tradition, whereby Gilbert Island males were capable of extraordinary feats of endurance and courage.

The people of Kiribati proudly believe their own martial arts were the forerunners of and the blueprint for the other great schools of martial arts that evolved later in Asia, including the Japanese Samurai martial arts and the Chinese Kung Fu. Kiribati legends say that their great hero Teraaka introduced and spread the Tungaru martial skills to other countries.

The Academy imposes a tough regime on its students, although not as harsh as the traditional warrior training of earlier days. As well as exercise and martial activities, the young men build their own houses, dig wells, collect coconuts, cut firewood, carry all materials, and cook their own meals.

**BELOW -** *In Kiribati, the Martial Arts Academy on Tarawa Island teaches the students something of ancient traditions.*

The boys learn the parts of the body that are vulnerable to attack, and how to defend them. They learn the entire warrior system of blows, kicks and strikes. Real weapons are used during training. The master, Waitea, believes they will know no fear when confronted with the real thing if they have trained properly. If an attacker carries a knife or a deadly weapon, a properly trained student will handle it easily. Students injured during practice are treated with tribal medicines.

More important than physical learning, however, is the knowledge they gain of traditional values and of the gods and heroes of their mythology. This invests their training with a profound significance. Nothing will ever seem futile or unreasonable to them and every action they make will be invested with meaning and with a spiritual depth. These traditions bring responsibility through every stage of life, even to death.

The Martial Arts Academy is run by the master Waitea, who insists on observing traditions. His father was a master too, who collected and researched traditions. Waitea uses his father's collection like a bible. The very land the Academy stands on has deep traditional significance.

Old rituals such as the purification ceremony before fighting are still used at the Academy. In the past young Gilbertese men had a ritual purifying magic called 'kauti'. They would face the rising sun at dawn and wash in salt water. From the sun came the power a warrior needed. Waitea also expects students to develop literacy skills along with their physical abilities, and time is given to teaching.

~

Ataria, one of the boys from the Academy, has followed the whole rigorous training programme. "They train us hard," he says. "But that was always the way for young Gilbertese men. We were thought of as warriors from earliest childhood. We always had to undergo extreme toughening procedures. The martial arts were studied by our ancestors too. We may practise slightly different methods today at our academy, but the codes of honour are the same. Our gods are still the same. We still believe in the power of magic and prayer."

Ataria is starting to see the bond between the past and the present. Like many of the island people, he accepts equally the techniques of training and the help of the supernatural in the form of gods, spirits and magic. Although there is a veil of invisibility between the real and the spirit world, the people believe that sometimes a fortunate individual makes contact with this other world. Ataria became aware of the spirit world through a strange experience.

Ataria's extraordinary adventure with the spirit world happened one day when he had finished his training and was walking through the jungle. Suddenly he heard an eerie sound. It seemed as if the jungle darkened. Now a clashing and banging could be heard. It grew in volume and Ataria, trying to trace the origin of the noise, peered through the bushes.

He saw a ghostly warrior in full traditional battle costume beating off an intruder. The intruder was getting the worst of the fight. Ataria curiously took another step and snapped a twig. The warrior turned his head and with a dark intense stare looked straight into Ataria's face. Ataria was pierced with fear. This was a ghost from the past. This was an active warrior from the spirit world.

Ataria could not contain his fright. He jumped back. Turning, he ran and ran until he arrived back at the Academy. He was in a state of shock. He found his master and breathlessly and still frightened he poured out his story.

"I have seen a ghost. He was a warrior from the realm of spirits. The veil of invisibility to the spirit world has been lifted and I am filled with fear. The warrior was dressed in full traditional costume. His suit of armour was woven from links of coconut fibre like chain mail. His helmet, which rose to a pointed dome on his head, was a dried blowfish. It gave him the stature of a sea god.

"Do you remember that one of our myths tells how the sun and moon were made from the eyes of a fish? The warrior has piercing eyes full of dark light from the sky and sea.

"He was fighting when I saw him and he was powerful with the armour of his ancestors and the years of his knowledge. He has the strength and mystery of other worlds. His gauntlets were woven fibres set with pointed shark's teeth. He was frightening."

Waitea calmed Ataria and smiled. "Don't fear our Warrior," he said. "He's been around here for a long time. Many of the students claim to see him. Perhaps he is at home here in this place of modern warriors."

"Is he a real ghost?"

"Who knows these things? You are living a similar life to the life he once lived. Perhaps you are imagining him. Perhaps he's watching you young boys and he's proud that the spirit of courage and discipline still lives on in Kiribati. He is like a guardian of the old traditions. You are fortunate to have the spirit of a warrior ancestor enter your mind. Just work hard and try not to disappoint him."

Ataria calmed down. He became very interested in the warrior and found out everything about him. He went looking for him but couldn't find him again.

The training at the Academy is not easy. After all, it is meant to give the students a complete education in the warrior arts. While Ataria was training and jousting with the other boys he imagined the hard life the warrior endured in his own time. Training in the past was far more strict than his own life in the Academy. It imposed on those ancient warriors a long and cruelly demanding programme from boyhood to young manhood. They lived like warrior monks for many years and served a hard master.

Ataria became nervous as the time for his graduation came closer. He had not seen the warrior again but now he was part of all Ataria's thinking. He told himself the warrior's story many times. It helped him prepare because he hoped to pass from the Academy with honour on his day of Tiotanga, his graduation day.

Ataria reminded himself that the warrior had had a much harder time in his traditional graduation to manhood. He would have had his hair cut with a shark's tooth and his face burned with the flames of his ceremonial fire. The shark's teeth would have punctured his scalp until his face was covered in blood. He had to endure severe tests of strength and endurance. Through all this, he lived in isolation.

The warrior would never have been allowed to show any sign of his pain in all his years of training, but he learned many important things. He learned the laws and myths of his people and the lasting power of his gods. He learned the ways of the weather and the stars. He learned the spells to make him brave and the spells to overcome his enemies. His ancestor spirits helped him pass through his rituals.

"I will remember all these traditions, " thought Ataria. "They are my heritage."

Ataria was right about the hardships of a boy's upbringing in traditional Gilbert Island fashion. At the age of five a boy was taken from the company of women and girls, and from the age of eight he learned, alongside his father, all the manual skills of house and canoe building, fishing, hunting and fighting, together with the rituals and magic that attended each activity.

At the age of ten he was adopted by a guardian, usually his grandfather, and from him he learned all the other traditions of his people. In return he became a devoted and totally obedient attendant on the old man. As he grew older he was kept in strict isolation and given many harsh tests of endurance, which he had to bear without complaint.

~

The day of Ataria's graduation was approaching. He had done well in his long training and Waitea was pleased with his work. Now there was the ceremony and the testing in the performance of the graduation jousts.

For many days beforehand the students made long and careful preparations. First they swept all the ground. Then coconuts were collected. The students then carried the huts for the gods into place, because the gods would be with them and it is important that the huts are placed in the right direction.

"We have huts for the gods of the earth and sea and the underworld," said

Ataria. "We have the huts for the god Nareau and for the gods Tabuariki, Auruaria, Nei Tituabine, Teweia, Riki and Nei Tewenei. They will be with us on our day of Tiotanga."

The students begin their elaborate purification ritual. First they climb the trees and collect coconuts to make an oil for anointing themselves. Then they gather certain bitter herbs and crush them and mix them with water to make the liquid for the final cleansing.

"Our master will give us the signal," Ataria reminded himself. "Then we must bathe three times in the sea. The gods are watching to see our rituals. We must follow the right precedure. Everything that happens today has a special meaning for us.

"Soon the visitors will arrive. Our families will come to see our graduation. I am nervous. Waitea wants me to wear traditional costume. My family will be there watching. The gods will be watching. Maybe the warrior will be watching. I must not dishonour them. I must remember all my training. The boy I fight is strong. I hope I am not defeated."

Ataria has completed his purifications. Now he is dressed in his traditional grass skirt and arm bands and woven crown. The sun is strong. He enters the jousting field, where the huts of the gods surround him.

The boy he is fighting lunges at him with a knife, and the movements of attack and defence begin. The fight is real and no allowances are made. Blood flows from the opponent's hand. The sun flares in their eyes and they are tiring, but still they fight.

Suddenly there is a loud cheering. The fight is over. Ataria has won. He has performed well today and has passed his graduation.

He looks among the visitors to see his parents' proud faces and there on the outskirts of the crowd he sees the warrior. Their eyes meet. Ghost or imagination, it doesn't matter to Ataria. He sees him clearly. He feels part of the continuity of a great tradition.

The warrior smiles approvingly at Ataria then vanishes into the crowd.

**LEFT -** *The traditional warrior lived a life of discipline and harsh training, from early boyhood to manhood. He lived like a warrior monk.*

# RITES OF

**A**ll through the Pacific, island societies are moving towards preserving and, where possible, renewing or revitalizing their ancient traditions and customs. In Samoa, an ancient cultural tradition is becoming part of the present.

# COURAGE

## TRADITIONAL TATTOOING
## IN SAMOA

**ABOVE -** *The tattoo is extremely painful, but pain is an essential part of the tradition.*
*In the course of healing, the newly tattooed men must keep washing and squeezing the patterned flesh*
*to reduce inflammation and infection.*

The tale of this tradition centres around Samoan-born Suluape Petalo, a dedicated teacher and the vice-principal of a major Samoan Catholic college. But he also has another life in a totally different world. Suluape is a leading artist and a craftsman in the age-old tradition of tattooing.

Suluape's family has long been involved in this tradition. His father and brother were well known as leading Samoan tattooists. As a young man, Suluape decided to champion the revival of this ancient custom. He believes that traditional tattooing gives Samoans a powerful sense of their identity and a new sense of pride and self-esteem. It is interesting that many of Suluape's clients are Samoans who now live abroad. There are large populations of Samoans living in the United States and New Zealand. Some of them return to Samoa in the sense of making a pilgrimage, to undergo a major event in their lives, a full traditional tattoo.

There is nothing like this in the Western world, and in fact nowhere else in the Pacific is tattooing performed in this traditional way. It was once considered a sign of status, and Suluape believes it still confers status today. This is not an eagle on a sailor's bicep or a small area of decoration that can be applied with relatively little pain with an electric needle. This is a full body tattoo, which, for a man, starts below the knees and covers legs and buttocks, extends over the stomach and back and finishes just below the ribs. Women's tattoos cover a much smaller area of the body, on the legs from below the knees to the top of the thighs. In both cases, the use of an electric needle is definitely unacceptable.

Application of a full traditional tattoo is a very long and extremly painful process. It is performed as it was in ancient times, with the correct traditional instruments. The pain is considered an essential part of the process—and it may take eight days or even eight months. Suluape was tattooed by his uncle when he was 17, over a period of one year.

There are cases of men who simply could not stand the intense pain, and left with the tattoo unfinished. Many must feel like this, but to leave halfway through a tattoo is considered a great disgrace. A complete tattoo is therefore a symbol of courage.

The tattooing of a young man was once a ritual of special significance, marking his entry into manhood. In earliest times only the chiefs and their sons were permitted to be tattooed. Similarly, women's traditional tattoos, called malu, were only available to the daughters of chiefs. Later the practice extended to untitled people, and now anyone can share this tradition.

In early missionary days, however, the practice of tattooing largely died out. The Church strictly forbade tattooing, regarding it as a heathen practice. In those days, teaching in a church college and practising as a tattooist would have created an impossible conflict. Now the Church is much more tolerant. It has even been known for a priest to be tattooed. Suluape maintains that Christianity is always more stable if it is in harmony with indigenous cultures.

There are many reasons given as to why this large-scale body tattoo has become popular again in Samoa. Suluape says it is a quest for the Samoan identity. The tall Samoans, a proud and once adventurous people, are great orators. Their traditions are passed down orally, and formal speech-making is highly prized. As their sense of tradition is of profound importance, a man is more likely to be chosen to speak if he is traditionally tattooed. Suluape holds two titles of orator.

The great writer Robert Louis Stevenson, who made Samoa his home and the Samoan people his own people, wrote of their strength of purpose and inherent nobility. The tattoos both confer nobility and make a direct link to their ancestors. One recently tattooed man said, standing almost naked, that he now felt fully clothed.

A full tattoo is usually planned in eight stages. Because it is such a drawn-out painful process, it can take a month or more to recover. Painkillers or drugs are

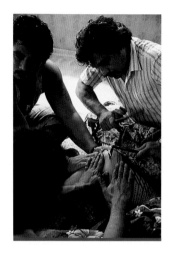

**ABOVE -** *The sharp teeth of the comb are tapped into the flesh with a short wooden mallet.*

**PAGE 80 -** *The traditional tattoo of Samoa is unique in the Pacific. This is a full body tattoo that, in the case of a man, starts below the knees and covers legs and buttocks, extends over the stomach, and finishes just below the ribs.*

**RITES OF COURAGE**

unacceptable as the experience and awareness of pain gives the tradition its full meaning. Watching a man being tattooed in the traditional fashion makes it quite clear that it is indeed an act of courage. He lies on the floor with his head back, his forehead perspiring, quite often grimacing with pain but rarely letting more than a moan or a sigh escape. Areas such as the kneecaps and inner thighs are particularly painful.

The dye for tattooing is made from soot and ink. The soot is collected by scraping the sides of a tin can heated over a fire. In the past the soot was obtained from the burnt inner sides of a nutshell, the Moluccan nut. The soot is mixed with ink made from the seed of the candlenut tree. It is then strained.

The teeth of the tattooing combs are made from boar's tusk or bone. The combs are fastened to a piece of tortoiseshell and attached to a wooden handle. It is important to keep the teeth sharp. A set of instruments can include up to 12 tools of varying widths. The narrow combs are used for fine detail. The broad combs, which may have 60 teeth, are used for the large dark areas of the tattoo.

The tattooing comb is dipped into the dye, and the sharp teeth of the comb are then tapped into the flesh with a short wooden mallet. The ink enters the skin as it is punctured. Apprentices pull the skin taut so that the tattooist can follow the straight lines he has previously marked out. Another apprentice constantly mops up the blood from the punctured flesh. This would be a daunting sight for anyone about to undergo a tattoo.

The constant fast tapping of the mallet has a relentless, nightmarish sound. The men being tattooed say that at night, in bed, the tapping sound resounds in their heads.

In the course of healing, the newly tattooed men must keep washing and squeezing the patterned flesh. Apprentices help. When the cold water first hits the tender flesh the gasp of shock is audible. The skin is raised in welts at first, but the squeezing and purification reduce inflammation and infection. They also help to establish the clarity of the ultimate design.

The black designs stand out clearly on the honey-coloured skin of the Samoans. Darker-skinned people could only achieve the same results with scarification or body painting. Tattooists employ traditional designs composed of symmetrical patterns, but no two tattoos are the same. Suluape sometimes experiments with new designs. Patterns can be based on animals or plants, the rafters of a Samoan house, or the curve of a canoe.

Families are very important to Samoans, and knowledge and traditional skills are handed down through the generations. Suluape hopes that one of his children will inherit an interest in the art of tattooing.

It is not wise to apply tattoos before the body is fully grown. Tattoos applied to a boy who is too young will result in the patterns and designs on this living canvas being distorted when he grows. Once it was considered wrong to display tattoos, and a woman is supposed to never show her tattoo in public unless she is serving at a traditional kava ceremony. These days, many wish to reveal both their bravery and their sense of tradition.

It is customary to have a celebration on the completion of the tattoo. Today's

LEFT - *When the tattoo is complete, there is a ceremony to celebrate the event. The tattooed men are like wounded warriors.*

celebrations are a much modified version of the great feasts of old. Long ago, when tattooing was permitted only to the families of the chief, the chief would send for the tattooist, or Tufuga, when he wanted his son or daughter tattooed. Strict daily procedures and rituals were followed, and at the end of the tattooing there was a dedication ceremony and a huge feast. The Tufuga was always deeply honoured and presented with fine mats of great value.

Today, the tattooed men, the leading villagers and the tattoo artist gather in the meeting house. The newly-tattooed men walk painfully with legs apart and unbent. They come like wounded warriors bearing a proud stigmata. They lower themselves to the floor in evident discomfort but they are garlanded with flowers and their faces are full of pride in their new feeling of being whole and complete.

The apprentices conduct purification rites. They break an egg over the head of each tattooed man and anoint them all with coconut oil during the ceremony,

Now follows the presentation of fine mats to the tattooist, just as in ancient times. This has always been one of the highest traditional forms of gift-giving and honouring a Samoan, and fine mats are still greatly prized today.

The tattooist is still regarded with the greatest honour. He is accorded the same status as a chief and is well paid. Outside the meeting house, the caller acknowledges the gifts and the money paid. But Suluape's real reward is to restore to Samoans a true sense of identity.

In a modern world that has discarded so many traditions and rites of passage, there is little opportunity in everyday life for a man to take on the role of a hero. The tattooing of the Samoan male is, for him, a symbol of bravery and manhood. The tattoo changes his life. It gives him a new meaning. He may contine to live an ordinary life, dressed in everyday clothes. But he now wears, for as long as he lives, the clothing of courage.

**R I T E S   O F   C O U R A G E**

# A MEMBER OF

*One of the creation myths of Kiribati concerns Nareau, the great creator god. Nareau was he who walked alone in the darkness before the first dawn, and he who fashioned the first man and woman from earth and water. Nareau so loved canoes that he decided to build one for himself. When he had finished it he was delighted with its beauty. It was such a fine and graceful canoe that he thought it should be preserved forever. So he decided to turn it into a new land. He created the island of Tarawa, whose southern part is like a canoe and northern part like a sail.*

# THE FAMILY

## THE CANOES OF KIRIBATI

Just as the violin or guitar of a great musician becomes an extension of himself, so the canoe becomes a part of the Kiribati fisherman. He handles it with a natural skill and confidence; he knows every detail of its behaviour under any circumstances; it is part of his life and his thinking; it is a member of the family.

Every family in Kiribati has a canoe. "A family without a canoe is a family in disgrace," said one young fisherman.

On the narrow low-lying atolls of Kiribati the sea is never far away and the men are considered to be among the world's greatest seamen. Even today more than eighty percent of Kiribati people live traditional lives, particularly in the outer islands. Most fishermen could not afford the expense of Western materials, so canoes are still made in the old traditional ways. Besides, "We still believe in our myths and traditions. They work better for us in our life."

When a boy is born, some portion of his umbilical cord will be taken and fastened to the prow of a canoe if it is decided that he will be a fisherman.

But it seems that apart from its usefulness, the canoe represents something deeper for the seamen of Kiribati. They are full of admiration for the canoe itself. The beauty of its lines and shape pleases them, and they derive great personal pleasure from the way it looks and the way it performs. Seamen of skill, courage and curiosity, the Kiribati in their outrigger canoes with sails value elegance and speed as much as the fishing capacity of a boat. Freedom and the feeling of flight have always been great human pleasures.

~

The canoes are on average 24 feet (7 m) long and about 2 feet (60 cm) wide at the widest point. The mast is supposed to be three-quarters of the length of the canoe body. Racing canoes vary in length and can, when handled with skill, reach astonishing speeds.

Kiribati boat builders are famed for using no nails or glue to make their canoes. They are lashed together with special hand-made rope. Today you can still see the gnarled hands of the old women rubbing and twisting the coconut fibres to make the sinnet or rope to lash the canoes together. Great skill is used in tying the knots. Canoes are even named after some of these special knots.

"Names carry an extremely important meaning for us," the young fisherman explained. In earlier days a man would live in solitude and abstain from all the pleasures of life while he thought deeply about the name he should give to his new canoe. Canoes must have names because they are living spirits. The I-Kiribati name them well, as they have always been people of vivid and poetic imagination.

"How fast it goes is very important to the naming of canoe, particularly if it is a racing canoe." said the young man. "Canoe racing is still a favourite sport in Kiribati and our canoes are very fast. We might call a racing canoe 'Fast as the Wind' or 'Swift as a Bird' or 'Flight of the Seabird', or we might call it after a cloud."

The islands of Kiribati are both fragile and limited, so the islanders extend their world to include the sea and the sky. Their ancestors were great navigators and understood the sky. Clouds are important and each different type, such as dark clouds and thunder clouds and clouds with lightning, has a name.

"We might call a canoe 'Nangi Ro', which means dark cloud," continued a canoe builder. "What that really tells people is—this canoe is dangerous. It's like a threat, or a cursing of all other canoes. You might as well give up now, it is warning. You can't compete with a canoe called Dark Cloud."

~

The making of a canoe follows traditional steps. First, the right place to make it must be found—a place blessed with good fortune, near the family dwelling. A thatched roof is raised over the building site, longer and wider than the canoe. Screens of leaves surround it.

In the old days a man would sleep beside his canoe while it was being built. This was partly to guard against strangers who might learn his secret methods of construction, and partly to stay near a precious object which was growing in his affection.

The right trees must be cut. At least four different species are used for various sections of the canoe, including the breadfruit, calophyllum and coconut trees. Trees do not grow very high on these islands, but it still takes a considerable time to cut and dry and dress the wood. In earlier days it was all done with an adze made from sharpened shell, and a kind of rasp and sandpaper made from dried stingray skin.

The stem of the boat is made first. It curves up at either end, and holes are pierced in the wood for the sinnet to be lashed through. The entire complex construction is governed by traditional procedures, which are apparently quite different from boatbuilding customs in other countries.

The structure of the outrigger presents problems, as no timber grown locally is buoyant enough for the float. Beachcombers hope for wood from other shores.

The sails on most canoes today are canvas, but in the past they were made from pandanus leaves pounded into flexibility and then sewn together. Some modern canoes are made using Western tools and skills, but not everyone can afford to do that. To make a canoe in the traditional way takes many months of hard work—but that makes them more valuable to the people.

When the canoe is finished it is given lengthy rubbings of coconut oil to protect the wood. There are sometimes ceremonies for the future safety of the canoe.

~

In the early days some families of Kiribati seamen were entitled to wear crests, rather like the heraldic devices of European knights. Most of these have stories and legends attached to them that tell of the adventures of gods or ancestors.

In Kiribati recently a large ocean-going canoe was constructed. Called a baurua, this type of vessel is rarely seen today. It was once more popular, and may have been the way the Gilbertese (as they were then called) first came to these islands. The canoes were often 80 to 120 feet (25–35 m) long—impressive structures. But the Kiribati fisherman and seamen are content with their own type of canoe. One that is a part of their everyday life; one that they can make a member of the family.

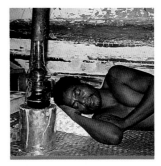

**ABOVE -** *A man might sleep beside his canoe while it is being built. This is partly to guard against strangers learning his building secrets, and partly to stay near a precious new object.*

# THE HEART

**A**ll over the world since the beginning of time, rituals, sacrifices and offerings have been made to the gods to ensure a bountiful harvest. People who live close to nature know that the gods must be appeased and their favour sought for anything as crucial to life as a good crop.

# OF A MAN

## LAND DIVING ON
## PENTECOST ISLAND

**PAGE 90 -** *The men of Pentecost Island in Vanuatu make death-defying leaps from the top of a high tower as a gift to the gods to ensure a successful harvest. The tower is built in the shape of a man.*

**RIGHT -** *A legend lies behind the breathtaking land dive. It started when Tamalie fought with his hardworking wife, Melu, and threatened to beat her.*

In the past, prayers, treasures, animals, food, and even human sacrifices have been offered. The gods will look kindly upon, and accept, only what is most precious to the supplicant. It must be a sacrifice of great value, or an achievement reached only with pain or extraordinary effort. The gods know what is expected of them. People must know what is demanded of them.

In many lands the harvest ritual involves an altered state. To make a sacrifice one must be prepared, purified, and profoundly aware of what is happening. In this heightened state the supplicant enters the domain of the spirit world.

In the case of the men of Pentecost Island in Vanuatu, their sacrifice, their gift to the gods, is a spectacular act of courage. They make a death-defying leap, a dangerous plunge from a high tower which can be more than 100 feet (35 m) above the ground. All that stands between them and certain death are the liana vines lashed around their ankles.

The Pentecost land dives take place only during April and May, to ensure a successful harvest of yams. In the weeks before the harvest festival, the divers undertake rituals of purification and make ritual protections to ward off evil spirits. When they leap they must be prepared.

No scientific means or modern equipment are used to build the diving tower or to assess measurements, stresses or tolerances. No nails, wires or ropes are used. It is all done with natural materials and by traditional methods—which, fortunately, are amazingly accurate.

The tower is built around a suitably tall living tree. It is a piece of complex engineering in which the structure is braced horizontally with crossbars. Hundreds of logs and branches are lashed together with thousands of feet of vines.

A series of launching platforms is built into the tower at varying heights. The earth under the tower is softened in case of accident. The length of the vines tied to the ankles is calculated carefully, with the vines' elasticity taken into account. They must stretch from the platform to the ground, less the length of the body. No recognized measuring device is used. The arms are kept out or folded during the leap so as not to be broken.

The diver's head almost brushes the ground as he snaps taut at the end of his upside-down flight. Sometimes one of the vines breaks, but apparently very few cases of death or injury have ever been reported.

Only males make the jump, including quite young boys. Women are forbidden to even approach the tower. Divers leap from various heights. Each jumper makes his own small platform and chooses his own vines. Individual platforms are designed to collapse at the end of the fall. A successful jump is celebrated with roars of delight. The land dive is a test of courage and manhood.

How did this dangerous and exciting custom begin? There is a legend well-known throughout Pentecost Island that tells the origins of the land dive. There is a surprising twist to the end of this old tale.

~

Long ago on Pentecost Island, a villager called Tamalie had a hard-working, gentle wife called Melu. Melu endured a great deal from her husband, for he was a bad-tempered, ungrateful, brutal man. She didn't mind his selfishness, or his drinking kava all day with his friends. It was his bad temper and his cruelty she couldn't bear. She tended the crops, gathered the firewood and made all the meals, and yet he was constantly shouting at her.

One day she returned after exhausting work in the field when Tamalie started angrily berating her for laziness. He insisted she return to the garden and bring back more food for his friends. Suddenly it was too much to bear and Melu at last lost her patience. For the first time, she shouted back at him and told him she was fed up with him and would not cook for his friends.

He exploded in fury. Screaming and raging, he picked up a large stick and ran to beat her. Melu knew this would be no ordinary beating. She had never seen him so angry. She feared for her life, so ran as swiftly as she could into the forest.

Through the darkness of the overgrown trees and into the sunlight she ran, stumbling and half falling but not daring to stop. Tamalie, still incensed with rage, ran after her and soon began to catch up with her. Melu's fear sent her running faster. The branches caught at her and the trees seemed to be spinning by, and still the pounding of Tamalie's feet and the rough increasing anger of his voice pursued her through the forest.

Suddenly in front of her in a clearing loomed a huge banyan tree, towering and twisted like a grotesque temple. Within its climbing roots and branches were small dim tree-caves. Melu knew that finally she could not outrun Tamalie. The old tree seemed like a refuge. Perhaps she could hide somewhere in the branches.

**ABOVE** - *Tamale chased his frightened wife to the top of a great banyan tree. There was nowhere left for her to go.*

She climbed the tree as quickly as she could until she found a hiding place. Looking down through the gnarled branches and hardly daring to breathe, she saw Tamalie come into the clearing.

Tamalie knew Melu could not be too far away. He looked everywhere—and then, fierce and sharp-eyed, he looked up into the trees and saw her hiding in the gloom of the banyan branches. Snarling with fury, he started climbing the tree. She could see his contorted face coming closer. She knew there was no escape.

Melu looked up helplessly. She was almost at the top. She climbed to the highest branches with Tamalie relentlessly following her. She edged up the last branch, tying a vine around her ankle as she climbed. Finally there was nowhere else to go. She shivered with fear. When Tamalie's swollen, screaming face was almost close enough to touch and his hand was reaching, grasping for her—she jumped.

Tamalie, lunging out after her, almost blind with anger, lost his balance and fell. He crashed through the branches and fell face first into the earth. He was killed instantly.

But Melu hung in the tree, the vine still attached to her ankle. She was bruised and her grass skirt was torn. She could hardly believe she was still alive. She could not have been sure that the vine she tied to her ankle in desperation would actually save her life. Such a thing had never been done before.

She untied the vine and climbed down. She regretfully examined Tamalie's body. There was nothing anyone could do for him anymore. Melu sadly walked away—but perhaps her heart was a little lighter at the thought of a life without Tamalie's anger.

~

This legend is widely known on Pentecost Island. Some say the spirit of Tamalie still lurks in the banyan tree. But a new and extraordinary event had been created by Melu's daring jump. Now, although it is a ritual demanding tremendous conscious courage—the bravest test of manhood, which in turn ensures the approval of the harvest gods—the fact remains that the first Pentecost land diver was a woman.

Perhaps one of the most moving aspects of the harvest ritual is the diving tower. It is constructed symbolically in the form of a man. There are the knees of a man, the low platform from which the children dive. There are the chest and the shoulders and the head of a man, and from these platforms the great flights are made. Inside the spaces of the chest the courage dwells, and both there and within the diver is the heart of a man.

**LEFT -** *Melu worked hard in the garden all day and carried home the firewood. Driven to despair, she attempted a dangerous feat.*

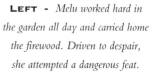

# RIDING

**T**he champion surfers of Tahiti claim that the Pacific Ocean and the Polynesian are one person. "We grow with the ocean. Surfing came from our past and it stayed in our blood all these centuries. Tahiti was the foundation of all surfing. Migrations began from here and took it to Hawaii and through the Pacific."

# THE WAVES OF HEAVEN

## HOW SURFING WAS BORN IN TAHITI

**ABOVE** - *The legend begins with a meeting of the mighty gods of Tahiti, who were thought to live in the towering mountains.*

**PAGE 96** - *The Tahitians believe that surfing began in Tahiti. The legend tells how the king, blessed by his shaman and riding his great long board, became the first man to surf.*

There is a secret to surfing, they say, as well as skill and discipline. To be brave. Never to fear anything. Not even the biggest waves.

The Tahitians believe that the exciting freeflying joy of surfing—the ecstacy of riding fast on the edge of a great curling wave; the art of balancing one's body and bringing it in tune with nature and the sea; the ability to stand erect like a god on a speeding surfboard—all this began in Tahiti.

Captain Cook may have been the first Westerner to witness Tahitian surfing. He wrote in 1777 after watching a man surfing: "I could not help concluding that this man felt the most supreme pleasure while he was driven on so fast and so smoothly by the sea."

Later James Morrison of the *Bounty* wrote about the amazing skill and dexterity of the Tahitian surfers, both male and female. In a lengthy description of surfing he wrote: "In a surf running to a prodigious height—they choose where the surf breaks with most violence, sometimes a mile from shore—they keep themselves poised on the surf so as to come in on top of it with amazing rapidity . . . they swim out again towing their board with them . . . at this diversion both sexes are excellent."

In those days, boards were sometimes much longer than the present surfboards. They ranged in size from 7 to 14 feet (2–4 m), some even reaching 18 feet (5.5 m), and could be very heavy. But even the heavy boards were managed with skill.

In the early 1800s, however, the missionaries, arriving on the island and seeing naked men and women engaged in such a pleasurable sport, were horrified. They felt surfing was an unfortunate heathen custom and forbade the sport. It languished for many years.

In Tahiti today there is a modern version of the medicine man, wise man or high priest of traditional times. He is called Raymond Graffe. A cultural advisor working at the Museum, he is covered in Tahitian tattoos and dresses in traditional clothing. Graffe has steeped himself in the authentic lore of Tahiti, re-enacted traditional roles and organized ceremonies on the island. It is all done in a passionate conviction that Tahitians must return to traditional beliefs to bring power and meaning to their lives.

"In time there will be a revival," says Graffe. "Men will surf like gods again. They will put aside all material values and embrace the old Tahitian ways. Then their surfing would be more focused, more disciplined, more powerful. They must call on the life force of the ocean. They must empty their minds of material things and fill their minds with the potency and strength of the gods."

There is a reason Tahitians know that the sport so loved all over the world began in Tahiti.

It was a gift from their gods.

~

It all began long ago, back in the beginning of time when the world was first formed. In the heavens above Tahiti, there was a great meeting of all the two hundred gods that made up the pantheon of Tahitian gods.

First came Ta'aroa, the creator and father of all the gods. Then came Tane the powerful god of the ocean. Next came Oro the fierce god of war, then followed all the other gods.

And if these gods looked a little like the towering mountains on the islands of Tahiti—those dark jagged mountains often crowned with a halo of clouds—it was because they were too awe-inspiring to describe in detail. Besides, the mountains follow the law of life. The gods do not lie down. They stand up. They stand tall like the mountains.

Hine Tepo Temerama, the goddess of the moon, was at this great gathering of the gods. It was decided at this meeting that the gods of Tahiti would give the gift of flying on the waves to the people of their islands. They would call it surfing. The gods decided that Hine Tepo Temerama should come down from the moon

and take on the shape of a mortal woman. She would go to live on the earth in her human disguise and teach the people this new wonder. She would live in the forests of Mahina. The gods would now call her Hina, goddess of the waves.

Hina walked through the forest. From the branches of the moon tree, seeds had fallen to earth. From these the forests had grown. She must find a tree with a strong life force to make the first earthly surfboard. She called on a medicine man to perform the right ceremonies. There were two trees to choose from, the Atea or sacred tree and the Uru or breadfruit tree, also a sacred tree.

They chose a strong Uru tree and the medicine man made his prayers. He blessed the trunk of the tree. At the right time of the moon the tree was cut down and was formed into a long board for surfing. The board was rubbed to get rid of the marks of the adze. Then it was polished with bark until it had a smooth surface.

But the board was far from ready. There were other important ceremonies to be observed. The board had to be blessed and consecrated and all traditional rituals observed. A board had been made that must become a sacred triangle—a union between man and the sea and the gods.

Hina sent word to the king and his court bidding him to come to the ceremony to dedicate the board when the day and the moon were right. Then she would show him an amazing thing.

A long procession set out for the sacred marae. It passed the stone statue of the ancient goddess and proceeded to the sacred stage. First came the high priest, followed by the king. Both men wore feathered headdresses and red maros (loin cloths). Red was a sacred colour worn only by high priests and kings. The lesser chiefs wore a yellow maro.

The king was followed by two men carrying the new board upright like a god. It must not touch the earth. Water must be its first ground. The musicians followed, then the king's brothers and finally all court members.

Hina was waiting at the top of the steps of the sacred marae. The musicians performed with drums and flutes and made music that evoked the sounds of the waves. In an elaborate ceremony, the board was blessed and dedicated to the gods.

Now the procession moved to the beach, with the board still carried upright. Here on the beach the high priest made his incantations to Tane the god of the ocean, while attendants with baskets of flowers threw them gently into the sea. The king knelt and received his blessing.

Hina showed him what he must do, and the king paddled out to find the waves. The chiefs watched in suspense. At last the king caught a wave and came flying in upright and triumphant. He was the first man to surf. From the shore Hina watched. From above the gods of Tahiti looked down. They were well pleased.

Today surfing is still a strong sport in Tahiti. In 1990 a young Tahitian, Heifara Tahutini, became the world champion. He is a shy young man from a simple Tahitian family who learned his skills from his father, riding the waves in all weathers near his coastal village home.

Raymond Graffe believes Tahitians will be world champions again. "In time there will be a revival. They will put aside all material values and embrace the old Tahitian ways. Then Tahitians will surf like gods again."

**LEFT** - *The first long surfboards were difficult to handle.*

# MODERN MYTHS

*When we forget traditional myths, we desperately create new ones to fit our age,*

*to cope with life, and to keep open areas for our spiritual development.*

*We create modern disguises for the mythic wisdom of the past.*

# THE FIERY

*Who is the mysterious John Frum? Nobody really knows, and yet he is the central figure in a powerful cult that has taken hold on the island of Tanna over the last fifty years and become an unusual modern myth.*

# MESSIAH

## THE JOHN FRUM CULT

**ABOVE -** *The sacred volcano Yasur on the island of Tanna, with Lake Siwi. Still active, the volcano rumbles and thunders and provides dramatic fireworks at night. This is the setting for the cargo cult based on the mysterious John Frum.*

**PAGE 104 -** *Followers of John Frum plant a cross, the symbol of Frum, on the rim of the sacred volcano, Yasur. They believe that Frum and his army live within the volcano.*

Tanna, a beautiful and richly fertile tropical island situated south of the New Hebrides group was, until the Second World War, an isolated little world of its own with a large Melanesian population. A high mountain range runs through the lush vegetation of the plains and valleys, with the highest peak, Mount Tukosmeru, over 3,000 feet (900 m) high. On the eastern coast of the island, rumbling, bubbling and flaming, is an active volcano, the sacred Yasur.

The spectacular Yasur, with the yellow Lake Siwi underneath, showers sparks and red hot rocks and at night provides viewers with firework displays. Frequent earthquakes and thundering volcanic eruptions make this and the nearby Sulphur Bay a picturesque site for a mythical being to emerge. There is no questioning the effect that a dramatic elemental force such as fire, erupting from deep within the earth, must have on an imaginative people. Sulphur Bay was one of the first villages to accept John Frum, and today is a centre for the movement.

Until the turn of the century the Tannese had openly believed in magic. It was a strong central force in their lives. They had magic stones that possessed great powers. This belief in magic has never really vanished from their lives. They were reportedly the most difficult people in the Pacific to convert to Christianity. By the Second World War, however, most of the Tannese had apparently been converted, mainly by the Presbyterian Mission, the first to arrive on the island. The Mission and English District Agents administered law and order on Tanna.

But then John Frum arrived on Tanna, and many of the islanders reverted to old ways of thinking. The John Frum cult is a 'cargo cult', which means that the god or hero of the devotees will come and bring them a better life with great gifts of wealth and material goods.

**ABOVE -** *A flag-raising ceremony is performed every day for John Frum. Many of the John Frum rituals are derived from military practices. The American army was based on Tanna during the Second World War.*

The cult of John Frum is said to have been developing since 1930. In 1937 John Frum 'appeared' at Green Point, and people came from all over Tanna to see him. Perhaps Frum would not have seized the minds and emotions of the Tannese so strongly if it had not been for the fact that Tanna was used as an American base during the Second World War. The American troops arrived laden, by Tannese standards, with every conceivable luxury. These rich goods, together with their weapons of war, constituted very strong 'white magic'.

As the Tannese had been treated as inferior by many Europeans, it also helped that the cheerful, friendly Americans treated them as equals and had many black soldiers among their troops. About this time, the John Frum movement assumed many of the trappings of military America. Today the John Frum leaders wear colourful, almost theatrical, uniforms, often put together from epaulettes, any kind of decorations or medals, old army badges and belts or hats. Their symbol is a large red cross, which may be a combination of the Christian cross and the medical red cross used by the army. The island is now dotted with these crosses, usually surrounded by white picket fences. There is a meeting house for John Frum in the village, and outside the meeting house John Frum flags are run up daily as a special ritual.

**ABOVE** - *There is a headquarters for the John Frum followers. The leaders of the John Frum movement dress in a style based on the American army uniform.*

At the heart of this new mythology is the belief that John Frum is the reincarnation of an ancient god. Some say he is the present form of the ancient god of Mount Tukosmeru, Karaperamun. Some say John Frum lives in the fiery vaults of the volcano Yasur, together with a huge, fully equipped army. They equate the power of the volano with the might of John Frum.

The neo-pagan John Frum movement first came to official notice around 1940–41. It was like a revolution among the islanders: churches, missions and schools were abandoned and the Mission villages were deserted. The island people went back to their old traditional customs of dancing and to the forbidden practice of kava drinking.

Kava is a narcotic and a hallucinogen. It is the root of the plant *Piper methysticum*, which grows to a height of 6 feet (2 m) in the jungle. Kava ceremonies are held all through the Pacific, and it is an integral part of many celebrations. On many islands, using it involves a whole formal procedure which must be followed. Islanders chew pieces of this root into a pulp and then mix it with water. It is usually made freshly

**ABOVE -** *Many of the people of Tanna believe that John Frum will return. There is a church for John Frum, where prayers are said and offerings are made.*

**THE FIERY MESSIAH**

and has a direct effect on the brain. Unlike many drugs it seems to have few adverse side effects. Kava drinkers are not aggressive or violent. The drug just leaves them feeling numb.

John Frum rituals evolved as leaders who 'met with' John Frum brought back the messages that would form the basis of the cult structure. Great celebrations and dances took place regularly, and John Frum flags were hoisted every evening. The Tannese began to get rid of their money, as John Frum told them that everything should be free for them. All money must be used up or destroyed. Some threw it into the sea. At one stage, people of Tanna broke into a European store, not to take anything but to remove all the ticket prices from the goods.

The movement developed and grew. John Frum pretenders emerged among the islanders. Later, Frum became less accessible and said he would send his sons to represent him. The government even tried to wipe out the Frum movement by imprisoning or exiling the leaders and punishing many followers. Despite several incidents over the years, the cult endured and spread to outer islands. It endures to this day.

On Tanna there is a church for John Frum where ceremonies are held, offerings are made, prayers are said, and John Frum songs are sung. There is a priestess who constantly composes new songs, some of which are sung to the tunes of old American battle songs.

Occasionally a group of Frum believers will climb to the top of the volcano carrying a cross. It is a long climb and the figures dragging the cross up the steep slope look like participants in a modern crucifixion. They plant the cross on the rim of the volcano, and if the sky that evening is full of fire and showers of sparks light up the sky, it must seem to them that Frum is aware of their mark of respect and has answered them.

~

Why did the John Frum movement evolve? Why is it such an indestructible myth? There are many possible answers, some based on political, psychological and social considerations. Others are not so easily explained.

The island people longed for independence. They wanted their own interests represented, they wanted a powerful god of their own. Perhaps they found the missionaries too strict, and resented their authority; perhaps they were not yet ready for Western culture and, as believers in magic, needed a power that could match the strength of white magic.

The figure of John Frum has unquestionably absorbed much of Christianity. He is a Christ-like figure who preaches love without imposing the prohibitions of the missionaries. The Tannese believe he is God and will come again.

John Frum has been claimed to be both white and black, American and Tannese, to be one person or another. He has been seen and he has, equally, never been seen.

Perhaps we shall never know who the real John Frum was, or if indeed he ever really existed. It is a mystery—but a living mystery. For many Tannese he still lives,

**ABOVE** - *John Frum followers running across the ash plains below the volcano Yasur.*

and is waited for today. He is like the very spirit of the islands, a powerful force that flows with the Pacific through their lives.

John Frum is, most movingly and amazingly, an act of the collective imagination of the people of Tanna. His story has earned a unique modern place in the pantheon of gods created since the beginnings of time.

**LEFT -** *The symbol of an invented religion which obviously owes something to Christianity.*

# THE FISHERMAN

**T**here is a creation myth told of the long stretch of islands that lie, isolated and fragile, in the equatorial waters of the central Pacific. It tells how, back in the beginnings of time, an ancester fisherman caught a large moray eel which lived in the reef. The eel begged for life, so the fisherman flung it across the sea, where it became the narrow twisted islands of Kiribati.

# AND THE EEL

## THE SEA PEOPLE OF KIRIBATI

It is not surprising that creation could begin in this way for these people, when fishing is the very life support system of so many of the islanders.

Until quite recently, the islands of Kiribati (pronounced "Kiribas") comprised four separately titled groups of islands in the central Pacific. To the northwest lay the major group, the Gilbert Islands, with the equator running through the middle. To the south were the Ellice Islands, and to the northeast the Line Islands. The Phoenix Islands were situated in the central area southeast of the Gilberts. In 1979 the independent Republic of Kiribati was established, which included all these island groups.

**PAGE 112** - *The fishermen of Kiribati set out with their eel trap. They will weight it with sinkers, bait it, and leave it in the depths for a day or two.*

The fishermen of remote Kiribati are renowned as being among the most fearless sea people of the Pacific. They live in harmony with their environment, and their kinshop with the sea is absolute. Their life is spent on the ocean and on narrow low-lying atolls that rarely, at any point on the islands, rise more than a few feet (1 m or so) above sea level.

Today, with the potential greenhouse effect, the I-Kiribati live in a world at risk, where the smallest rise in ocean levels would drown their low-lying islands. Their world could easily vanish completely. But the sea is part of their lives, and their sense of the continuity of nature is part of a life force that has become the very key to their survival.

Recently, a true-life adventure occurred that potently illustrates this point. It might very well be called a modern myth.

~

On 18 November 1991, three fishermen left their village on Nikunau, one of the islands of the Kiribati group. It began as an ordinary fishing trip. Seven months later, on 11 May 1992, they finally made landfall in Western Samoa.

The three fishermen had run out of petrol, and strong winds had swept them out to sea. Early in the journey the boat had capsized and they lost all food and equipment. They had nothing but a piece of rope and a hard hat they found floating by. The ordeal that followed—in an open boat, exposed to the elements—is one of the great modern epics of survival.

In a situation where the average person would not survive even a fraction of this time, the fishermen had faith that they would live. In the village of Tambametang on Nikunau their families never stopped believing that they would return.

The epic journey of these Kiribati fishermen was soon picked up by the world press. Their courage and endurance created a new record of survival at sea. Two of these quiet fishermen became modern heroes. The third and eldest, having endured for so long, died in the last weeks of the journey. On landing, the survivors were taken to a Samoan hospital where they soon recovered.

For half a year they had suffered heat, exposure and privation on a journey of over 1,500 miles (2,500 km). They collected water each night in the hard hat and they caught fish, including shark with its highly nourishing liver, using the piece of rope. Only their skills and their long familiarity with the sea enabled them to endure this remarkable odyssey.

The two Kiribati fishermen and their families who waited are true traditional sea people of the Pacific. The clue to their amazing story of survival lies in their ancient ability to live fearlessly with the sea. The fishermen instinctively became a living part of the sea, accepting without resistance the flow, the drift and the currents of the ocean that would finally bring them home.

Just as there are many myths concerning the fishermen of the Pacific, so there are many eel myths. One famous eel creation myth concerns the first ancestors, who lived in darkness because the sky was wrapped tightly around the earth. A meeting was held to decide how the sky could be prised off the earth and raised above it. Riki was the tallest of the ancestors, so he pushed the hardest when they attempted to lift the sky off the earth.

The giant Riki finally raised the sky up into its present place. His arms remained

**ABOVE -** *When the fisherman has made his house-like eel trap, he will smoke it as part of a traditional ritual.*

**RIGHT -** *The fisherman anoints his eel trap with coconut milk and prays to his ancestors that the eels will always find his trap inviting.*

in the heavens and became the Milky Way. His body fell to earth and shattered into many pieces. These fallen pieces of the ancestor Riki became the eels of the Pacific.

The first mythic eel of Kiribati lived out in the reefs surrounding the islands. Today, the islanders still fish the reefs for eels. They are caught in traps of different sizes which, in many villages, resemble miniature woven houses with a pointed gable roof.

In the small villages of Tarawa Island, the capital of Kiribati, traps are still made traditionally. It is a craft that has been handed down through the generations. Making the traps begins with ceremonial rituals and magic. The fishermen call on the spirits of their ancestors to make their traps inviting and they entreat the spirits to always make their catch abundant.

The house-like traps are made from the wood of the pemphis tree, a prolific tree that grows near the shores. The wood is cut into strips and soaked in seawater to make it flexible enough to weave. The base of the trap is made first and the cross pieces rise up to become the sides. The corners and intersections are bound and lashed together with coconut fibre string.

For the roof, a split branch becomes the central ridge pole and the sloping woven sides are again lashed to the walls of the eel house. In the front, a round doorway or access hole is left for the eels to enter. This entry has a cleverly constructed woven channel so the eels cannot escape. An opening hole with a closed flap is made in the roof to remove the eel.

When they are finished, the traps are smoked over a small fire. Later a coconut is split and the milk is poured over the traps to anoint them.

The traps are baited with octopus, so the fishermen and their families set out at night with lamps to catch the bait. This is quite a lively occasion. In the shallows under the stars, lit only by lamplight, the octopus hunt has a theatrical edge. When an octopus is caught, the fishermen and their wives and children kill it by the rather grotesque custom of biting its eyes out. They then turn the octopus inside out, using their mouths and hands. The long silvery tentacles dramatically grip the arms and grasp and splay across the faces of the hunters.

The eel traps are taken out beyond the reef and baited. There are platforms on the sides of the traps for sinker stones, lashed on to weight the traps. The traps are then lowered to the depths, where they will hopefully entice the eels. The fishermen leave the traps for one, sometimes two nights.

They return full of anticipation, anxious to see if a guest has been lured into the eel house. There is a high rate of success with this method. The eels, which can be up to 3 feet (1 m) long, can be aggressive. Eels have rows of sharp and vicious teeth. The fishermen are well aware of this and are very careful when drawing out the long plump eel.

Eels are regarded as a delicacy in the villages. They are cooked in a traditional underground Kiribati oven, and served coiled up on a woven leaf platter.

In the steps they follow from the making of the traps to the cooking and eating of the eels, the people are living out the traditions of their ancestors.

And so the cycle repeats itself. Long ago the myth of the fisherman and the eel was created out of a need to be part of nature, and the people are still sustained by this belief. It is the ground they walk on and the food they eat. It is a link to their ancestor spirits and part of the energy of their daily life.

**ABOVE -** *The eels are cooked in a traditional Kiribati oven.*

# THE ARRIVAL

*This tale is about the creation of a modern myth in world art. It is also a love story that is perfumed with the essence and the flavours—the noa noa—of Tahiti.*

## A PAINTER DREAMS A MODERN MYTH

Two men who were to become famous in the creative world of Europe came to the Pacific in the nineteenth century. Both were great creative spirits and both left their mark forever on this part of the world. One was the Scottish writer Robert Louis Stevenson, and the other was the French painter Paul Gauguin. They were to become part of the story of Pacifica forever. Both, in different ways, were myth-makers themselves and were eloquent writers and men of imagination and vision.

They were similar, perhaps, in the power of their genius, but totally different as people. Robert Louis Stevenson came to the Pacific to give his love and support to a whole race of people. He came to die, to embrace the death he had long awaited in a warm land. Gauguin, in contrast, came with a passion to live, to renew himself, to break open the doors of paradise, and reveal the warmth and magnificence of it to the world.

Paul Gauguin's arrival in Tahiti in June 1891 was, in a sense, an arrival for the whole of nineteenth-century European painting: he carried the dreams of other European artists with him. Art would never be the same again and the way the world was seen would be changed forever.

The controversial Gauguin was a sensual, passionate artist responsible only to his vision. Although he helped change the course of art, fame and fortune eluded him until after his death in 1903. Although he influenced the painting that came after him, his own age was not ready for him and his new kind of perception and energy. He died in poverty in the Marquesas Islands.

Born in Paris of a French father and a Peruvian Creole mother, Gauguin spent the first years of his life in Peru. He became a sailor and later a successful stockbroker in Paris. He married and had five children. Having painted part-time for some time, he eventually left his business life to paint full-time. From then on he struggled to survive; he could no longer afford to support his family and left his wife and children.

His extraordinary painting life among his now-legendary artist friends, particularly "my friend Vincent" Van Gogh, is another story. Our tale begins in 1891 when Paul Gauguin set out for Tahiti. "I am leaving to find peace," he said, "to rid myself of the influence of civilization. I want to create art that is simple. To do that I need to renew myself in unspoiled nature."

Gauguin sailed into Papeete, the capital of Tahiti, and for the first time saw the breathtaking view of nearby Moorea just before dawn from the water. Moorea, opposite Papeete, has one of the most magical mountain ranges of any Pacific island. On a fine day the whole beauty of Moorea floats in front of Papeete like the dwelling place of the ancient gods. Gauguin wrote: "For 63 days I have been on my way and I burn to reach the longed-for land." In Tahiti he was to find the form and hues of his art, and the way to transform himself and his perceptions.

Gauguin's whole life and art had been a journey towards this heartland where he was to create a body of paintings of blazing intensity. During his time in Tahiti he also wrote and illustrated his now-famous journal. It is fortunate that a great artist and a fine writer kept such an intimate and sensual account of his daily life. Witty,

observant, and moving, his diary was called Noa Noa, for he was intoxicated with the heady perfumes of Tahiti. There was a girl who would open his eyes anew for him. So Noa Noa became a love story, a glowing love story that spun a golden light around Gauguin's days in Tahiti.

Disappointed in Papeete, he left the town and set out to the unspoiled villages to forget his European self: ". . . well and truly destroyed, all the old remnants of civilized man in me." Gauguin embraced Rousseau's dream of the 'noble savage' and believed that humans were part of nature and should return to this condition.

Gauguin journeyed around Tahiti and at Taravao, at the far end of the island, the local people invited him to come and eat with them. Among the people, Gauguin met a woman who asked him where he was going. On the spur of the moment he said he was going to find a wife. The woman said she would give him her own daughter. Is she young? Is she pretty? Is she healthy? Gauguin wondered as he entered the hut and sat down to wait. He was served a meal of wild bananas and crayfish.

**ABOVE -** *Manao Tupapau ("Spirit of the Dead Watching"), by Paul Gauguin. This is a painting depicting a true incident with Tehura.*

**T H E   A R R I V A L**

Perhaps he was not serious at first about acquiring a wife, but all this changed when a tall young girl in pink muslin entered the hut. Gauguin's description of his first sight of Tehura is memorable. He had come to paradise and here, in Tehura, was his Polynesian Eve. She seemed golden to him: transformed by Gauguin's imagination, every long crinkled hair on her head seemed to glitter. "In the sunshine she was a riot of chrome yellows." Gauguin asked her if she was afraid of him and whether she would come and live with him and be his wife. She agreed.

"My heart beat faster—this girl, this child, charmed and scared me—what was going on in her soul? this object of gold that I loved already . . . I felt a shy hesitation about signing this marriage contract so hastily thought of." Gauguin was worried about their age difference. He saw in Tehura the independent pride of all her race and had some fears as they left for his home. Her mother asked him, "Are you kind? Will you make my daughter happy? In eight days let her come back. If she is not happy, she will leave you."

Gauguin wrote: "My new wife was not very talkative. A week went by. I loved her and told her so. She asked me to let her return to see her mother as I had promised. To me it seemed like goodbye. Would she come back?" Several days later, Tehura returned.

Gauguin was in love and from his brush flowed a stream of paintings full of brilliant and improbable colours that blazed with light and life. Each one has become a famous landmark in the history of painting.

"I set to work again and happiness succeeded to happiness. Every day at sunrise there was a radiant light in my dwelling. Everything shone with the golden light of Tehura's face. Everything exhales the noa noa of Tahiti . . . The two of us would go simply, naturally as in paradise to refresh ourselves in a nearby stream. Every day Tehura yields herself more and becomes more loving. I am no longer conscious of the days and hours. When I am working Tehura instinctively keeps silent."

Gauguin was convinced that there were certain qualities in lines, forms, and colours that would express every human emotion—"a great emotion can be translated instantly, dream about it and seek for it in the simplest form." One of the examples of a painting with great emotional power that he did at this time is his Manao Tupapua (Spirit of the Dead Watching). It came about in the following way. One day Gauguin went out, leaving Tehura at home:

"One day I had to go to Papeete. I had promised to come back that same evening. On the way back the carriage broke down half-way. I had to travel the rest of the way on foot. It was one in the morning when I got home. Having just recently run out of oil, my stock was due to be replenished, the lamp had gone out and the room was in darkness. A kind of fear came over me and a terrible suspicion. Surely the bird had flown.

"I struck matches and I saw there on the bed Tehura, naked, motionless, her eyes wide with fear, gazing at me as if she didn't recognize me."

Gauguin comforted her as she cried for him never to leave her alone without light. But for Gauguin, in that flickering light, an image had burned into his mind,

an image that would become one of his most famous paintings. A naked young Tahitian woman is lying on her bed, flat on her stomach. Her terror-stricken face is half-turned. A strange, dark figure sits by the bed like the personification of her fear. A mauve to violet background floats with flowers. Her bed is covered with a dark blue cloth printed in yellow. Over that is a sheet of yellow. "Yellow is the colour that creates within the viewer a feeling of the unexpected. It also creates the illusion of a scene lit by a lamp. The background must seem a little terrifying; violet is the just right colour. The only thing I see is fear."

At night on the beach Gauguin and Tehura used to look at the stars together. In the clear air and the darkness, the points of light blazed with the same intensity as Gauguin's paintings. "The stars interest her greatly. She asks me what the morning and the evening star are called in French. She finds it hard to understand that the earth goes round the sun. She tells me the names of the stars in her language and the myths behind them."

Gauguin suffered from jealousy. One day when he went fishing with the men of his village, he caught a huge tunny fish. The fishermen laughed and whispered in Tahitian. Gauguin insisted on knowing what amused them: they told him that when a man caught a fish by its lower jaw, it meant that his woman had been unfaithful to him. Gauguin confronted Tehura.

"'How was your lover today?'

'I have no lover.'

'You're lying. The fish has spoken.' Her face took on a look I had never seen before. She prayed aloud. Her prayer done she said with tears in her eyes, 'You must beat me or you'll be angry for a long time.'

"Before that resigned face and that marvellous body, may my hands be forever accursed if they scourged that masterpiece of creation. Naked like that she seemed clothed in the orange-yellow mantle of purity . . . a beautiful golden flower which I worshiped as an artist, as a man.

"I kissed her. It is by gentleness that anger must be conquered. It was a tropical night. Morning came radiant."

Tehura was the model for the memorable paintings that Gauguin created during that time of driving creativity in Tahiti: The Delightful Land; Woman with a Mango; The Ancestors of Tehamana (Tehura) and many others. When the time came for him to leave his paradise, he realized he would probably never know such calm and happiness again.

"I had to return to France—imperative family duties called me back. Tehura had wept for several nights. Now tired and melancholy, she sat on a stone letting her feet brush the salt water. The flower she had been wearing had fallen faded into her lap. She was singing this song as the ship carried us away. 'You will see the man who has left me . . . Tell him you have seen me in tears.' "

Noa Noa was published in 1901 in collaboration with Charles Morice. Gauguin's own manuscript was not published until long after his death. The paintings he did during his time in Tahiti were not a commercial success: it took time for the world to catch up with his genius. Gauguin finally returned to the South Seas in 1895, but not to his Tehura or to a dream of happiness. Constantly ill and frequently in hospital, he would never be well again.

In 1898 he was desperate and contemplated suicide. First, however, he would paint his "last will and testament"—his largest painting, a fresco like those of the Renaissance. He wanted it to be a symbol of the eternal questioning of the human race. He called it Where do we come from? What are we? Where are we going? The painting reads from right to left, from birth to approaching death.

"Before I died I endeavoured to paint it. I worked day and night for a whole month in an incredible fever. I do believe this is the best thing I have ever done. Before dying I put into it all my energy, such an aching intensity."

It became Gauguin's most famous painting. He resisted suicide and lived to paint more works, including the brilliant Contes Barbares (Primitive Tales), before he died in 1903 on the island of Dominique in the Marquesas.

Before he died, he wrote with defiant pride: "I had the will power to do things my way . . . I am a savage. But I feel I have been right about art. If my works do not endure there will remain the memory of an artist who set painting free."

**ABOVE -** *In his journal, Gauguin describes his own jealousy when the sailors tell him that catching a fish by the lower jaw means your lover is unfaithful.*

On another level, it was not only Gauguin the individual artist who helped create that freedom, but his early recognition that there were other worlds, other traditions, and a great natural force that art could tap into. Art has always represented the nourishment of the spirit in the world. It is the very fabric of myth that when European art was struggling to be freed of centuries of artistic convention and find new ways of seeing, the natural wisdom and life force of the Pacific should help bring about its regeneration.

**LEFT** - *"Now tired and melancholy, Tehura sat on a stone letting her feet brush the salt water." From Gauguin's journal, Noa Noa.*

# THE FESTIVAL

In the village of Kabaga, dreams are being spun: dreams of disguise and transformation from plain subsistence farmers to heroes; from ordinary villagers to splendid men clad in the hues and masks of heroic warriors. Tradition and creative energy are the power behind this transformation. There are dreams, too, of the Kabaga singsing group winning first prize at the Goroka Festival.

# OF DREAMS

## THE GOROKA SINGSING RENEWS THE HEROES

From inland, from the coast, from all points of the compass in Papua New Guinea, singsing groups, representing the traditional dances and performing arts of each village, are journeying to the biannual Goroka Festival. Their pilgrimage takes them to the Eastern Highlands; to the land of eternal springtime; to the region they call the Mountains of Heaven.

The Goroka Festival began in 1957. It rapidly grew into an almost legendary event and has become an occasion celebrated for its splendid performances and huge audience. People come from all over the world to see the amazing spectacle. It has become an inspiring event and a way of renewing old traditions. While festivals like this exist, the ancient cultures of the people of Papua New Guinea will remain a living force.

Anda, a young unmarried farmer of Kabaga, tells how the villagers prepare for the festival. They always put tremendous care and enthusiasm into their preparations, but this year they believe they really have a chance of winning one of the major and lucrative prizes offered for the best costumes and performance. Their village is poor and the prize money would be a great benefit to the people.

As part of the winning group, Anda might be able to afford a bride price. The young men must save their wealth if they wish to marry. The Kabagas must marry people from other villages: they consider they are all brothers and sisters of the same blood. Anda is a handsome young man, but even a man the villagers consider downright ugly will find a wife if he has sufficient wealth, which is measured in pigs and kina shells. Kina shells have always been so valuable that even today the Papuan currency is called kina.

But it is of course more than the prize money that drives the singsing groups. In the past these highland clans were almost constantly at war with each other. Men were traditionally trained as warriors, and it may be the memories of heroic deeds and war-dances that stir their creative energies. They feel the power of their past and manhood when clad in their full magnificence.

Anda shows how the men collect the plants and clay for their body paint and costumes. They dig for the clay, which is both white and orange. They will keep some paints as powder to mix when they arrive at the festival.

The group carefully unwraps its headdress feathers, which are very valuable and are kept for generations. The most prized feathers come from birds of paradise, small, bright parrots, or rosellas, while the long black feathers—usually seen on the top of the warrior headdress—come from the tail of the kush kush bird.

The men wear a wig as the base for their headdress. In the past the wig was made of woven leaves tinted with clay; now some of the men use a woollen cap. The wig used to be stuffed with human hair, but now it is filled with dry grass. When the feathers are added at the Goroka Festival, the headdress will become a crown of brilliant plumage.

The Kabaga villagers have saved up for a year to pay for the hire of the bus to take the Kabaga singsing group to the festival. Unfortunately, they could afford only one bus, although everyone in the village would love to go. Instead, they can take only 25 carefully chosen performers. But as they are convinced they will win, they feel they will soon have no more troubles. The first prize is 3,000 kinas and they hope to bring this rich award home.

Some of the 80 groups that have been invited to this year's festival will not be able to afford a bus. These groups may walk hundreds of miles to attend. If they are not Highlanders, they may have a long climb too: the Mountains of Heaven are some 10,000 feet (3,000 m) high.

But the Kabagas are making their journey in style. It is three hours' travel by bus through the superb scenery of the Southern Highlands to the Goroka Festival. They sing all the way, practising their performance. In a spirit of optimism, they improvise a song about themselves and how the judges will certainly see how magnificent they are, and that they surely deserve to win the prize. They are not entirely joking.

Part of the Kabagas' traditional costume calls for rare silvery leaves that grow only in a special place some miles from the village. So they stop the bus to find the trees and bear small branches back in triumph. The sun glitters on the leaves, reflecting light as they sway and blow with the smallest movement. It is obvious why these particular leaves are prized. Anda explains that they have their own style of movement in Kabaga. The costume of leaves must be properly displayed to give it bouncing, dancing life as the warriors move.

~

The bus finally arrives at the site of the festival. It is a huge area, as large as a dozen playing fields. This year there are 1,600 performers and there is already a buzz of activity from all the competing groups. The Kabaga singsing group sets up a camp for itself and now begins the serious business of the make-up and adornment. In dozens of other camps, other singsing groups are doing the same thing.

The men burn the bark of a tree to make the charcoal that gives them such a fierce look. They crush and moisten it for painting. They cook the orange clay until it turns red. The red clay is precious and is usually used to paint the nose and lips and sometimes the eyes. The yellow paint comes from a small plant called wandia that grows where there are landslides. No actor on a Western stage could take more care in applying make-up. For the Kabagas, the process becomes almost a religious experience. Every plume and stripe of paint has meaning as a symbol of their traditions.

The warriors of Papua New Guinea are transforming themselves, and they are artists in this elaborate act. Their imagination is prodigious as they each create a dramatic and theatrical masterpiece—their transfigured self. Representing their own past, they are creatures of light and darkness with their oiled bodies that shine with a glow that would frighten their enemies, and now must please the judges. Each warrior has a large crescent-shaped necklace of highly polished mother-of-pearl, a valuable and treasured possession.

After they have finished their preparations, the Kabaga mix with the other performers—both new and famous groups. Most warriors wear a nose decoration; through a hole in the septum of the nose, they may put a fierce-looking boar's tusk or feathers and decorations that may extend as much as six or seven times the width of the face.

One of the most famous of the groups are the Mudmen from the Asaro Valley. They coat their bodies with white or grey clay and cover their heads and faces with huge, frightening-looking masks. Sometimes pig's teeth are set in the mouth of the mask for added effect. The Mudmen re-enact the legend of their great victory where they appeared to their enemies in the gloom of the jungle, covered in pale mud, and frightened them into retreat. Some say their enemies thought they were an army of ancestor spirits, hence the enemies' terror.

The dance of the Mudmen is slow and measured and they appear from behind trees like angry ghosts. They have another-worldly look, like alien creatures from space or the demons carved on medieval churches. Their slow dance speeds up as they act out their tale. A convincing story, it is easy to believe how they would have terrified their enemies. Indeed, they still would be frightening to many people who had not seen them before.

Another well-known singsing group are the Wigmen from beyond the Wahgi Valley. They wear elaborate wigs of human hair, which may extend almost three feet (1 m) either side of the head and are topped by plumes of brilliant shades. Wives and children willingly sacrifice their hair for the men's wigs.

The Chimbu singsing group also has human-hair wigs. They are carefully made on a frame and can be dyed red or gold. Unlike the wigs that extend sideways, these fan downward like ancient Egyptian wigs. Their headdress often includes the entire turquoise breastshield of the superb bird of paradise.

The poor, brilliant birds of Papua New Guinea have faced many losses to keep the warriors in plumes. There are allegedly over a thousand different species of birds in the country, including the different species of the spectacular bird of paradise. The feathers of these beautiful birds are highly prized, particularly their magnificent tail feathers. Fortunately, the female's feathers are plain so at least half the bird population is safe. Feathers from the red-plumed bird of paradise are eagerly sought because red feathers are most desirable. Parrot and rosella feathers are also popular as they come in many bright shades, including pinks, greens, and yellows. The long

**THE FESTIVAL OF DREAMS**

black feathers of the cassowary, a huge flightless bird, are also prized.

Many of the groups have dances where they resemble birds with leaves that move like feathers. Some of the dances are very like the courtship dances of the native male birds. The dancers, like the birds, know that they are attractive to females in their bright costumes — another reason for their brilliant display.

Other singsing groups in masks from various villages imitate the movements of their totem animals, such as the crouching movements of the Frogmen and the hunting movements of the Owlmen.

A lost people are making their first appearance at this year's festival. They are the Hagahai tribe from the inland of Madang Province, who were only recently discovered. They will perform their age-old dances outside their village for the first time.

The clans and singsing groups are gathering now in the dancing fields. The energy is rising as painted bodies shake and stamp. The warriors cry out and shout with mounting excitement as they run or dance, their costumes coming to quivering, shaking life with their movement. Spears rise and fall, rattles shake, armlets of grass tufts shiver. Drums roll with an insistent beat and the dancing and singing begin. The festival grounds are like a great patterned mosaic of brilliant, singing rainbow hues.

As Anda watches the dancers in their dazzling costumes and hears the excitement of stamping feet, he feels a thrill of pride in the other tribes and their dances. It is almost as if he can feel their dreams too. He sees the dancers dressed as owls in eerie masks, one with a dead mouse in his mouth. He watches the Frogmen and the musicians painted white with clay. Here at the festival all their traditions are on display and Anda feels a part of his whole country.

As the heat of the day rises, the judges leave the grandstand and mingle in the crowd. Anda's loyalty to his village and his feelings of competition rise again as he realizes how much they want to win. There is an air of anticipation: who would win the valuable prizes? A silence falls as the winners are announced and the prizes presented. To Anda's great disappointment, his group does not win a prize.

As the festival fever dies down, the Kabaga group returns to its camp. Slowly, the men of his village remove their finery, their armbands and necklaces, their wigs and feathers, their headdresses and ornaments. Anda goes down to the river with his group to wash the clay from their beards and the bright make-up from their faces. When their first disappointment wears off, the men feel their spirits revive.

Standing in the river, his face washed clean, Anda sees the familiar faces of his friends emerge from their cleansing. He finds himself smiling: perhaps they haven't won this year, but maybe next time. Next time at the Festival of Dreams they might be the victorious ones. He sees the remembered reflection of his splendid painted face in the water.

In the meantime, the Kabaga men have all been lifted out of their mundane daily lives and, for a brief but memorable time, each of them has known what it is like to be a hero.

**THE FESTIVAL OF DREAMS**

# SPIRITS OF

The world of magic and the realm of the spirits have always existed alongside the daily life of the traditional people of Vanuatu. These people are aware of the existence of this other dimension. It is always there waiting for them. The people tread carefully through the forests: it may not be safe or correct for them to walk along the Path of the Spirits or under the shadows of the Tree of the Dead. These are part of the secret world that the people of Vanuatu acknowledge. This story is concerned with that world.

# THE DEAD

## A TALE OF MAGIC
## AND SECRET WORLDS

The people of Vanuatu have a different attitude towards death. They do not fear the dead, but respect the power they hold. The dead are still alive for them in another spirit dimension. They can be part of their life: the living may ask the dead to help them.

Old people can be thought of as being already partly dead. This is not an insult or an implication that their powers are waning. It really means that they are closer or have more access to the spirit world.

Skulls, the bones of the dead, and signs of death do not disgust or frighten these people. Instead, they regard them as physical symbols of the spirit world and include them in their life.

One of the customs until recently when someone died on Southern Malekula, an island of Vanuatu, was to prepare a funerary effigy. The mortuary effigy body was made of tree fern, wooden or bamboo base, overmodelled with vegetable fibre paste, then painted to represent the dead man's status in life.

~

The Vila Cultural Centre in Efate, Vanuatu, houses a rare collection of art objects. These reflect the history, myths and cultures of Vanuatu. Here there are strange sculptures of heads that are human skulls with an overlay of clay modelling. These heads have an eerie, timeless quality in their expressions, and a presence that is both human and yet of the spirit world.

Here are also masks, figures, sculptures, headdresses, plaques, and many other cultural works, gathered from the many different clans throughout the 80 islands of Vanuatu. Standing tall like wooden giants, the groups of often larger-than-life sculptures cast mysterious shadows and draw the viewer into another world. The museum is more than a collection: it is part of a strong, new spirit in the Pacific to keep alive an awareness of the cultures, traditions, and ritual objects of the islanders.

Many ritual objects are homes for the spirit within. This is the story of an unquiet spirit, a haunted carved and painted figure, thousands of miles from its homeland. It is the story of magic crossing the continents. It is also the tale of a man who knew how to reach the spirits of the dead.

~

Vianney Atpatoun, who was a cultural centre field worker based at the museum and is now head of the Malekula Cultural Centre, is a deeply spiritual man, steeped in the life of Vanuatu and knowledgeable about the beliefs and customs of the people. He was one of the first cultural workers in Vanuatu to film and record unique traditional events throughout the islands. His work documents and preserves the rituals and ceremonies of traditional life in Vanuatu.

Vianney has become a traveller on mythical paths. He journeys to the far corners of the islands to film, document, and record dances and ceremonies. Some of these are so secret that they are completely taboo and even he is not allowed to record or film them.

Vianney arranged to visit the island of Malekula. It is barely fifty years since many of these people gave up their practice of cannibalism. This custom had much

PAGE 134 - *The dances that follow men's secret grade-taking rites on Malekula in Vanuatu. They wear tall and elaborate headdresses made of carved, painted wood.*

LEFT - *A burial mound. Skulls and other bones of the dead do not frighten or disgust the people of Vanuatu. They regard them as physical symbols of the spirit world.*

more to do with the rituals of their life as warriors than satisfying hunger. Malekula is an island where magic is still very much a part of the lives of the people. Many of them still live traditional lives. Vianney went to film the dances that follow men's secret grade-taking rites.

The clan chief met him and led him into the hidden worlds of the forest, through ferns, vines and trees, past burial mounds where the skulls of the dead watch with invisible eyes and where the sun glistens on the leaves of high trees. Finally, they left the shadows of the jungle and arrived at a clearing. It was the sacred dancing field.

Around the sacred field stands a circle of large stones, some of which are almost as tall as a person. These are ceremonial stones placed there for commemoration. They chart the progress of a man through the stages and the gradings that he achieves in life.

ABOVE - *The small spirit figure was of the kind used to ward off evil spirits. It was a wooden sculpture painted in ochre, black and white.*

In the ceremony Vianney wanted to film, a new slit gong drum for dancing was to be initiated. A tall, partially hollowed tree trunk formed the body of the instrument, with bands of carved decoration. The large drum seemed alive with its carved face on top and the deep voice that resonated when the body was struck with drumsticks. Before it was played, it was ritually anointed with coconut milk and christened.

After the rites were completed, the men were ready to dance in celebration to the beat of the drum. The dancers are decorated with body paint and mostly wear very tall and elaborate headdresses like huge, pointed crowns. Made of carved wood, some of these headdresses have faces; some contain painted figures; and some have carved or woven spires billowing with tufts of grass and feathers. Together with their spears, the men seem like giants when they dance.

**SPIRITS OF THE DEAD**

But Vianney was not the first to document and film the dances and activities of his people. Our story of the haunted doll begins seventy years ago when an American couple, Martin and Osa Johnson, came to Vanuatu to record a glimpse of the people. It was a world that was, at that time, virtually unknown to most Americans.

The Johnsons were adventurers and early filmmakers in the 1920s. Theirs is an interesting story. With courage and imagination, they journeyed to remote and unknown areas of the world, including the Pacific islands, filming what was mostly rare and unusual footage in sometimes extremely dangerous circumstances. When they returned home, they aroused a great deal of interest and made a living screening their 'exotic' movies.

But they sometimes showed a very limited understanding of the different and complex world they filmed. To them, the people were 'savages', and they made little attempt to understand the values of the traditional societies they encountered. However, they had a bold documentary style and a genuine interest in the sculptures and artifacts of the people they filmed.

During their visit to Vanuatu (then known as the New Hebrides), they filmed dances and interviews. They took projectors and screens, showed films to the people, and then filmed their delighted reaction. The films still exist.

Vianney returned to the museum with his new dance films from Malekula and watched them, checked them, and discussed them with his colleagues. There are now 45 cultural workers in Vanuatu engaged in the work of collecting and preserving their traditions and ceremonies, so significant work is being achieved. Among this rapidly growing and important collection is rare archival film, including one of the early black and white Johnson films.

~

The small spirit figure of our tale was a wooden sculpture painted in ochre, black and white with outstretched arms, about 10 inches (25 cm) high. It was a figure of the kind used to ward off evil spirits and was worn tucked in the belt of a dancer. This spirit figure brought a strange twist to the story.

Vianney made a long study trip to America. It was an exciting adventure for him. He managed to visit many cities and saw many museums. He visited the Osa and Martin Johnson Museum in Kansas. Among the artifacts displayed there on a shelf was a carved wooden spirit figure that the museum had never been able to identify with any certainty. While Vianney was visiting the museum, an extraordinary thing happened. The spirit figure began to move and then to rock violently.

The museum workers asked Vianney if he could help them. He recognized the figure as coming from Vanuatu, from the island of Malekula. Vianney did not say so, but many people believe it is unwise to remove traditional objects from their place of origin. Even on a practical level, wood, in particular, can dry and split in different climates. At least in the controlled environment of a museum, physical damage is less likely to occur.

It soon became clear to Vianney what had happened. He explained to the museum workers that the Vanuatuan figure held a spirit and that the spirit was disturbed. Vianney also remembered that at the time he was in the museum discussing the figure, he felt a strong awareness of the spirit of Martin Johnson. He thought that the problem must somehow lie with him.

To calm the spirit figure, Vianney knew that he must visit the grave and contact the spirit world. He went to the cemetery in Kansas where Martin and Osa Johnson were buried. The people of Vanuatu traditionally speak to their dead. It is an accepted custom. It preserves continuity and often offers a special kind of help and protection to the living.

When Vianney arrived at the cemetery, it was a fine, bright day with a clear, blue sky. There were no shadows, howling winds, or gothic storms. Vianney stood in front of Martin's grave and quietly introduced himself, saying he was from Vanuatu. He said he had come to talk to Martin Johnson, and he established a communication between himself and the dead man. He reminded Martin Johnson of his long-ago visit to Vanuatu, and the link between them. He told him the story of the spirit figure. Having wished the spirit of Martin Johnson a lasting peace, he then slowly walked away through the fields of graves.

Vianney's communication worked. The figure stopped its rocking. The unquiet spirit was now at rest.

~

This may seem a strange tale to us in our Western countries, but in the forests of Vanuatu, the story of the haunted spirit figure is not so unusual. It speaks merely of a lost dimension, where mythology and magic are a part of everyday life.

**LEFT -** *Around the dancing field are the ceremonial stones, set there for commemoration. They chart the progress of a man through the gradings he achieves in life.*

# THE TWILIGHT

**U**nder the dark volcanic mountains of their islands, the gods of the Pacific had reigned over the lives of the islanders since the beginning of time. Their power was absolute. They controlled the processes of fertility— birth and death, growth and renewal. They were the gods of nature.

# OF THE GODS

## THE BLUE LAWS OF THE COOK ISLANDS

Passionate, mysterious and relentless, the presence of the gods was woven through the traditions and the daily life of the villagers. They gave a magic protection to villagers, strength to warriors, and meaning to all aspects of life.

When the Christian religion came to the Cook Islands there was a conflict between the moral standards of the Church and the urgent life force of the old gods of the Pacific. The Cook Islanders were a strongly sensual race of people, famous for the seductive beauty of their dancing.

Not all, but many of these nineteenth-century missionaries came from a strictly conventional social framework. It is not surprising that they found the gods of nature threatening, uncontrollable, and too powerful in their own environment. The sight of sculptural representations of strongly phallic gods was most disturbing to them on every level.

With a fanatical zeal, and in a very short time, they had converted whole island communities to a new set of values. An early visitor to the Pacific, the observant Victorian lady Miss Gordon-Cumming, once wrote with great insight that, as the Pacific Islanders had such imagination and lived so close to the invisible world of the spirit, it was not surprising that they accepted the invisible spiritual world of Christianity.

But acceptance was not enough for some of the the early missionaries, who were a product of their age. They felt that to give Christianity an enduring force in the islands, they must root out and destroy all traditional beliefs and customs as heathen. Only then would they have established a lasting control over the conspicuously 'pagan' nature of these people.

It was a sad and inflexible period of limited knowledge and misunderstanding between cultures and beliefs. Cannibalism, head hunting, and ancestor worship filled missionaries with horror—they had no understanding of why these customs were followed. They also feared the music and dance of the islands, and the sexual customs so different from their own strict world. It was this repressed world they wished to replicate in the islands.

In the Cook Islands the missionaries were excessively stringent, and forbade all song and dance and all signs of physical affection between young people. They imposed a set of harsh codes. They called them the Blue Laws.

These laws covered many aspects of daily life, and islanders could be prosecuted for many 'crimes', for example: being pregnant, if you were an unmarried woman; placing your arm about a woman; travelling to other villages on the Sabbath; card playing, and so on.

Fire and brimstone lectures, public disgrace, huge fines, and severe punishments were imposed. An enormous police force and an army of Church wardens were paid to catch offenders. This created an over-zealous army of vigilantes.

The islanders clad their dark beauty in white gloves and hats and prayed that the fire in their blood would be subdued. The old gods of the Pacific lost their power and receded into an endless twilight.

~

The tale is told of a girl called Maki who grew up in a small village on the Cook Islands. It was a place where the heart is content and each day has its meaning. The villagers lived a traditional life where work and play followed age-old customs.

Maki was a beautiful dancer, and it was said that when she danced it stirred the boys to feel love and desire for her. But she had already chosen her lover. His name was Tua and her dancing was all for him.

Then the missionaries came, and Maki was told she must follow the code of the Blue Laws. She must no longer dance. They told her that if she followed her old ways, the vengeance of their God would strike her.

The tale tells how the villagers secretly went up into the hills and met in a hidden place to hold their now forbidden celebrations. In secret they danced the Urupiani, the dance that invites love—nothing can halt the passion that rises from this dance. It had always been the prelude to love. Perhaps the old Pacific gods heard the dancing and, stirring in their sleep, emerged briefly from the darkness.

Maki and her Tua danced all night. In the morning they went to swim in the sea. The sea was fresh after a night of love and the waves reminded them of their dancing. Maki knew that Tua was her happiness and forgetting the Blue Laws they danced and hugged and ran hand in hand along the sand.

The severe terms of the Blue Laws saw dancing as a threat to the holy work of the missionaries and a manifestation of the devil in action. The wardens saw the happy loving couple dancing on the beach and arrested them. Maki was flogged and put in the stocks. Tua was flogged and made to carry a heavy stone right across the island.

For a long time these harsh sentences were imposed on the Cook Islanders who failed to abide by the difficult codes of the Blue Laws.

Now, a century and a half later, a new awareness presides in the Cook Islands. The Church now embraces the wisdom of tolerance. The Cook Islanders are once again proud of their heritage and deeply value their ancient Polynesian traditions. The Blue Laws are long forgotten and the spirit of the dance has been renewed.

**ABOVE** - *The harsh punishments imposed by the missionaries for breaking the strict Blue Laws included floggings.*

**THE TWILIGHT OF THE GODS**

# A ROYAL

In centuries past, the Tongans were the undisputed rulers of a large part of the South Pacific. They were the

most expert seamen, fishermen and navigators, and it is not surprising that one of their ancient divinities was

a great fisherman god named Maui. An ancient creation myth concerning Maui tells how he created Tonga

by a magnificent fishing feat. He pulled it, and all the surrounding islands, up from the bottom

of the sea on his fishing hook.

# TRADITION

## POLYNESIA'S LAST MONARCHY

For more than a thousand years, the 150 islands that make up Tonga in the southwest Pacific have been bound together as one kingdom. There is one language, and all the land is owned by Tongans. The people are proud and independent, and have never been colonized.

The first official Tu'i Tonga (king), Aho'eitu, began his reign in about AD 900, by which time Tonga had already established a traditional national government and administration. (Tonga had then been settled, some say, for as long as two thousand years.) The island monarchy had been established hundreds of years before some of the leading European monarchies consolidated. It was a well-organized and sophisticated society. It is said that the Tu'i Tongas are of divine origin, the original king being the son of the creator god, Tangaloa Eitumatupa.

In 1862 the renowned King George Tupou I of Tonga, having been converted to Christianity, gave all his people total freedom. He voluntarily ended his traditional and feudal powers and converted Tonga into a constitutional monarchy.

Problems followed during his reign, and that of his great-grandson George Tupou II, with European rival powers looking to control all island territories. Through Tonga's treaty with Britain, however, the last monarchy in the Pacific was saved and the constitutional monarchy remained firm.

In 1918 Tupou II was succeeded by his daughter, the celebrated Queen Salote Tupou III. She handled and helped stabilize the national and international problems of her country with patience, diplomacy, and a commanding presence. She is credited with bringing peace and prosperity to her country.

Queen Salote died in 1965, a world famous figure deeply mourned by her people. Now, for the first time in Tonga's history, the three royal dynasties of

Tonga's noble houses are united by marriage and birth in the person of the present monarch, King Taufa ahua Tupou. The motto on his coat of arms is 'God and Tonga are my inheritance'.

The Princess Salote Mafile'o Pilolevu Tuita is the only daughter of the present king. With her three brothers, she grew up in the white weatherboard palace overlooking the sea in Tonga's capital, Nuku'alofa ('City of Love'). The tall, gracious princess, who has inherited the famous charm of her grandmother Queen Salote, was the guide around the interior of the palace, and explained the traditions of the royal family.

It is a small, fairytale palace. Built in 1867, it is of decorative white weatherboard, two storeys high, with a small tower, a royal flag flying, and wide balconies all around. French doors and bay windows are left open for the sea breezes. The two front rooms are reception rooms, and the Privy Council Chamber houses the Tongan Constitution in a glass display cabinet. It is also hung with portraits and photographs of past royalty. Across the hall, the throne room looks like a plush but comfortable lounge room.

The domestic life of the royal family takes place in the other rooms and upstairs. The seafront palace will probably not last another generation as the structure has been damaged by successive storms and hurricanes.

Princess Pilolevu was brought up and trained by her grandmother, Queen Salote. From her she learned the old Tongan traditions and the rituals of royal behaviour, and that the Tongan people are deeply aware of the marks of respect that must be made in the world. One of the most widely recognized marks of respect for tradition is the woven mat garment, the ta'ovala that all Tongans, male and female, wear around their waist.

The great traditional treasures of the royal family are their tapa cloths and their fine mats. These are more precious to the Tongans than any crown jewels. At the coronation of the present king the great long tapa cloths were laid out along the path from the chapel to the palace. The tapas are made from mulberry bark, which is peeled from the tree, pounded, and put together and painted by hand. It takes a long time for the villagers to complete one of these cloths. The queen's mother looks after this valuable royal collection, which has been presented to generations of Tongan kings.

Of even greater value than the tapa cloths is the royal collection of fine mats. Fine mats enjoy great value and prestige on some Pacific islands, particularly Samoa. Royal mats are handed down from chief to chief, and some are antique. These are mats that have been used as garments. The Tongans believe they are alive—that they contain the essence of all who ever wore them.

The most treasured of these great mats have titles themselves, and bestow an aura of nobility on the person who owns them. Princess Pilolevu has an ancestral mat called Vala Tauo Tamasese. It is decorated with highly prized red feathers from the kula bird, and has tears and holes which do not in any way diminish its value. "We are blessed when we wear a mat such as this," explains the Princess.

Tonga has become an almost totally Christian country, and yet everywhere there is evidence of traditions and earlier beliefs. The innate spirituality of the people enables them to accept a 'new' religion.

Because it is right on the international dateline, Tonga claims to be the country that sees the first light of each new day. It is a magical island group that has, so far, preserved many old values and traditions. Tonga was christened the Friendly Islands by Captain Cook in 1777. It was an appropriate title.

~

In Tonga, on the main island of Tongatapu, there remains an unsolved mystery that goes far back in time. It concerns the great stone Ha'amonga'a Maui or, as it is also known, the Trilithon. It is said to have been built by an early Tu'i Tonga. The Trilithon is a famous landmark in Tonga and comprises three huge stones, each weighing about 40 ton/nes. They are set up like some mighty gateway, standing 18 feet (6 m) high. There is nothing else like them in the Pacific. Perhaps the nearest relation would be the great stones of Stonehenge. Scientists believe the Trilithon was built in the same way as Stonehenge and the Egyptian pyramids, with a ramp of earth to help drag the stones into position.

No one knows where the stones came from. They are not made from the local coral limestone of Tongatapu. However, the seafaring Tongans regularly made expeditions to distant islands. One theory is that they were brought back to Tonga by sea, slung between two canoes.

There are many legends about the Ha'amonga'a Maui. In one tale, the fisherman god Maui carried the stones of the Trilithon on his back. Ha'amonga'a Maui means 'the burden of Maui'.

This ancient monument is at least seven or eight centuries old and stands near the village of Niutoua, the old royal site of Heketa. The most popular and likely theory is that the Trilithon was built by the eleventh Tu'i Tonga, whose name was Tu'itatui and who ruled about AD 1200. He was a powerful but eccentric king who so feared assassination that he struck the knees of anyone who came too close to him. His name means 'King-strike-the-knee', and he supposedly built the Trilithon as a gateway to the royal compound. Two great kings' tombs are also attributed to Tu'itatui. These terraced tombs of the Tu'i Tonga are called langi, and were built up to hide the sacred burial ground from the eyes of ordinary people.

The present king, Taufa'ahau Tupo, believes the Trilithon was an astronomical device. He is supported in his theory by the presence of a V-shaped notch on the upper side of the lintel stone. He is convinced that the V-shape marks the winter and summer solstices, providing early Tongan people with both the means to plan crop planting and a time-scale for navigation by the stars. The king and his assistants carried out checks, and on the longest and shortest days of the year the bearings match the arms of the notch perfectly.

~

There is a renowned choir in Tonga, the Maopa Choir. Tongans are famous for their musicality and their fine strong voices. The members of the choir have an

**ABOVE -** *The long tapa cloths are laid out on the lawns of the palace. These cloths are of great traditional value.*

annual custom that on the king's birthday they sing to him in the grounds of his palace. Each year they sing Handel's 'The King Shall Rejoice'. Here, in this stirring work, is a symbol of the Tongan people which reveals their gift to a spiritual king and their natural acknowledgement of an earthly royal tradition.

**LEFT** - *Scene from an re-enactment showing one of the early Tu'i Tongas (Kings of Tonga) who may have been the builder of the Trilithon. The Tu'i Tongas have ruled Tonga since the ninth century.*

# REQUIEM

*The Scottish-born poet and author Robert Louis Stevenson became a legend of the South Pacific. In 1888, when he set out on two years of extensive travel through the Pacific Islands, he was already a famous writer. Works such as* Treasure Island, Kidnapped, *and* The Strange Case of Dr. Jekyll and Mr. Hyde *were among the most popular books written in English.*

# FOR A POET

## ROBERT LOUIS STEVENSON
## IN SAMOA

In 1890, Stevenson decided on the beautiful island of Samoa as the permanent home for himself, his American wife and his family. Here, beneath the mountain Vaea, he purchased a large tract of forest land and built a grand house overlooking the sea. It was given the Samoan name Vailima, meaning 'Five Waters', for the five streams that ran through the forests.

Stevenson's large white house still stands under the mountain in Samoa, the jungle still covers the slopes of Mount Vaea, and from the balcony the sea glitters in the distance. His grave can be found at the end of a difficult climb to the top of the mountain.

Stevenson was one of the very few white men who had come to the islands in the nineteenth century asking for nothing. He cared about his new country and its people, and from the beginning swore his allegiance to them and was prepared to give himself to them in total friendship. He wrote of Samoa:

> I love this land; and I have chosen it to be
> my home while I live, and my grave after I am dead.
> And I love the people and have chosen them to be
> my people to live and die with.

The Samoans did become his people, and he learned their ways and customs and to speak their language. The Samoans in turn grew to love and respect Stevenson. With affection they called him 'Tusitala', the Teller of Tales.

He explained to the Samoans that he had been born in a cold and distant country called Scotland, where he was a weak child. He had battled all his life with a great sickness called tuberculosis. He said, with joy, that in their warm and friendly world he seemed to be finding his health again.

Samoa was hardly known in the Western world at that time, except as a possible colony. It was the time of the great race for colonies and for Pacific wealth. Three powerful white nations—England, Germany and the United States—were battling for the islands of Samoa. There was also internal faction fighting among the three most important tribal chiefs.

Stevenson became friends with the chiefs, journeying to their villages to talk with them. He soon became involved in the politics of the Samoan islands and, with the future of the Samoans in mind, he studied all sides of the problems and advised accordingly. He watched and listened carefully, and in 1892 he wrote *Footnote to History: Eight Years of Trouble in Samoa*, which looked at the situation in the islands. Such a book was unique at the time.

Stevenson gave his complete concern to the people. The Samoans recognized him as a wise friend who cared for them, gave them his best counsel, and fought passionately for justice for them. They understood that he had great common sense and was also a man of honour.

The Samoans felt that Tusitala was now one of them. At the top of Mount Vaea he had chosen his final resting place. He would live in Samoa forever.

There came a time when the Samoan chiefs wanted to show their gratitude to Tusitala for his guidance and rare understanding. They decided to build a road to Stevenson's house, Vailima. They cleared the forest and planted an avenue of trees. They called it 'The Road of Loving Hearts', knowing that in time the saplings would grow and become tall native trees. They were writing their own living story in tribute to Tusitala.

~

In the meantime, Stevenson enjoyed his life in the warm tropical climate—writing, wandering through the forest, watching the birds, riding his horse. He never regretted his decision to settle in Samoa. He knew his time there would be short. Each day was a gift. He wrote: "If more days are granted to me, they shall be passed here where I have found life most pleasant."

Death came swiftly and kindly to Robert Louis Stevenson. He had lived under its shadow all his life, but he had lost his fear. He was resigned and at peace. His last years had been happy. He once said, "One loses one's fear of death in Samoa." He had also said, "Death. I have been waiting for you these many years. Give me your hand, and welcome." He was prepared. He had chosen his final resting place and had already written his own epitaph.

**ABOVE -** *In the warm tropical world of Samoa, Stevenson lived in reasonable health for the first time. The Samoans respected him and called him 'Tusitala', the Teller of Tales.*

**REQUIEM FOR A POET**

**RIGHT -** *A Samoan chief. Stevenson learned the Samoan language and was deeply concerned with Samoan affairs. He became friends with the chiefs and attended their meetings, giving them wise and practical advice.*

The news of the death of Tusitala spread swiftly through the island. It was the third of December, 1894. Stevenson was 44 years old.

All through that night, more than two hundred Samoans laboured to clear a path up the slopes of Mount Vaea. The sound of their axes rang through the island so that in the morning Tusitala might be carried to the summit and buried where he most wished to lie. He had been prepared for burial by the Samoans, who rubbed his body with oils and the fragrant flowers of the moso'oi tree.

The people came from the villages all over the island. They came to Vailima with gifts of flowers and fine mats to farewell Tusitala—and to mourn.

His family followed the coffin. His wife Fanny, who had kept a night-long vigil by his side. His step-children Belle and Lloyd, who made the climb to the summit. And his mother, who knew the unnatural pain of seeing her only child die first.

The low, mournful notes of the conch shell could be heard. The men had gathered coral pebbles and crushed lava rock for the Samoan grave. The chiefs were according him the highest honour they knew—the fanua loto, the grave for a royal burial. The fifteen chiefs of Samoa carried the coffin up the long mountain track to the high grave. After Stevenson's death, the mountain became a bird sanctuary and the chiefs tabooed the use of guns.

In the late nineteenth century, it was rare for a Westerner to take notice of the point of view of the islanders. But for once it was clear what the Samoans thought. They held their own silent requiem for the poet who had come to live among them as they toiled up the mountainside that morning after his death.

Robert Louis Stevenson
was unique in the history
of our Islands at this time.
He was a free creative spirit
who asked for nothing
except friendship.
He had no greed in his heart,
no wish to take or trade
or collect the bodies or souls
of his fellow men.

He felt no white superiority.
The Samoans were his brothers,
equal and free.

He respected us.
He honoured our traditions.
He gave to Samoa
the dues of a homeland;
his life, his concern
and finally, his death.

And because he bothered
to tread carefully into our lives;
And because he lived among us with wisdom,
We accord this rare man the honours of a chief.

But it was Stevenson's own epitaph that remained in the hearts of the mourners.

*Under the wide and starry sky*
*Dig the grave and let me lie.*
*Glad did I live and gladly die*
 *And I laid me down with a will.*
*This be the verse you grave for me;*
*Here he lies where he longed to be;*
*Home is the sailor, home from sea*
 *And the hunter home from the hill.*

# THE MERMAID

*In ancient times when the oceans were still being charted and the edges of maps held dragons, and beautiful creatures half fish and half human swam in the depths of the sea, a strange sea mammal called the dugong was thought to be a mermaid.*

# MAMMAL

## THE DUGONG OF PORT RESOLUTION BAY

**PAGE 156** - *Today, the only dugong living in Port Resolution Bay will come when called by someone slapping the water.*

*RIGHT* - *In the legend, Amela took her coconut shell containers down to the bay to fill them. It was here she saw the dugong for the first time.*

The dugong is of the order Sirenia. Does the name have an association with old romantic tales? The sirens, legend tells us, lured sailors to their death. Singing and calling, they drew them to the hazardous rocks. This tale is about a dugong that lives in the waters of Vanuatu in Port Resolution Bay.

In 1774 the navigator Captain James Cook was at the end of a long two-year journey from England through the Pacific. He arrived at the New Hebrides (renamed Vanuatu in 1980) and the island of Tanna. From his sailing ship, the 'Resolution', he could see the glow of the volcano Yasur, sacred to the people of Tanna, and was drawn to take anchor in the northern bay.

From this anchorage he charted the islands, aided by his newly developed chronometer. He made hundreds of observations and measurements, and his calculations were surprisingly accurate.

Cook was not a sailor to see mermaids. He was a man eager for the truth. This expedition was in the cause of science. But it is likely that there were at that time dugongs living in these waters. Cook named his anchorage Port Resolution Bay.

~

More than 200 years later, village life continues in Port Resolution Bay. The villagers are well aware of the dugong living in the bay. Once they might well have hunted him for food, but times have changed and the dugong is now a protected species. Because of him old stories are remembered.

There are many myths about the dugong. One of the stories belongs to this bay and the village. It happened long ago.

The women were sitting out under the trees in the village preparing their food and vegetables in readiness for cooking. They had no salt then, so the women cooked in seawater.

One woman, Amela, picked up her coconut shell containers and went off to collect salt water for cooking. Down through the village she walked to the bay. On the way she passed her husband Kasaro who was fishing off the rocks.

She waded to a shallow inlet and was just about to scoop up her salt water when she was startled by a large shadowy shape in the water. It was most unusual. It looked like a huge fish.

"Kasaro, Kasaro," she called loudly to her husband. "Come here quickly."

He came running with his fishing spear and, like his wife, was surprised to see the huge creature. He was soon balanced on the rock and poised ready to kill it.

"Stop. Do not kill me," cried the dugong. "My name is Kasaro, the same as yours."

The fisherman was so surprised he lowered his spear. As he watched, something strange happened. The dugong turned into stone.

Kasaro picked the large stone out of the water and placed it under a nearby tree. The stone dugong still sleeps there, under the tree.

Today, the dugong in the bay responds to humans. Reports say he is the only one in Tanna. The villagers fear for his loneliness and for the extinction of the species. Although it is protected, the dugong is still hunted for food on some of the islands. This situation is unlikely to change.

Some of the villagers regard their resident dugong rather as a pet. He seems to be quite tame and friendly towards them, although some fear his long arm-like flippers. If they were held by the flippers, even in fun, they could drown.

Splashing the water calls him in to play. He always answers the summons. He is obviously very aware of humans and appears to enjoy being near them. He arrives

**TOP** - *The dugong is a mammal of the order Sirenia. In earlier times the dugong was thought to be a mermaid.*

**ABOVE** - *According to the legend, the dugong cried out when Amela's husband, Kasaro, poised his spear to kill him.*

**ABOVE** - *Port Resolution Bay, on the island of Tanna in Vanuatu.*

quickly, the crescent moon of his whale-like tail speeding him along. He moves with pleasure in his underwater world, and comes up to breathe every few minutes in a touching reminder of our warm-blooded kinship.

The dugong will hear the splashing and come in to play even if he is grazing far out on the ocean bed. The hearing of the dugong is acute, although there are no signs of ears on his blunt-nosed head.

Dugongs are sometimes called sea cows, but the heavy skeletal structure is actually claimed to be most like that of an elephant—a strange elephant, without limbs or trunk. Dugongs can grow to 10 feet (3 meters) long and can weigh up to 1,100 pounds (500 kilograms).

The villagers believe the first dugongs in the bay came because they were following the canoes in from the sea.

~

As the sun goes down, the village people come in from their swimming and playing. The dugong at sunset seems partly human before returning to its undersea world.